Praise for the Author

"As the CEO of the Australian Physiotherapy Association (APA), it gives me great satisfaction seeing our members advocate for the health and wellbeing of the community. Physiotherapists live by the mantra of 'move well, stay well' and are well equipped to help the community stay physically active at all levels. Scott's book simplifies the sometimes complex nature of health and wellbeing and is a good resource for all consumers."

Cris Massis – CEO of the Australian Physiotherapy Association

---

"Who doesn't want to live a healthy and happy life?! Scott has put together an easy to read guide that I think everyone could learn from. For some, it may even be life changing!"

Angela Tsun – TV presenter

"This book will change your life for the better! Scott has written and researched all the elements you need to have a happy, healthy and fulfilled life. Easy to read and full of factual information on how you can achieve the happiness you desire. A book we wholeheartedly recommend."

Carly and Tresne – Founders and CEOs of The Happiness Mission

---

"Over the last decade or so, many thousands of words and hundreds of books have been written on the exciting new science of positive psychology and happiness. Few, however, touch on the integral link between psychological health & wellbeing and physical health & wellbeing. Scott Wescombe makes that connection in this book and what a great connection that is to make!"

Dr. Tim Sharp – Chief Happiness Officer of The Happiness Institute; Organisational Consultant and Speaker/Presenter; Executive Coach & Clinical Psychologist; Adjunct Professor – UTS Business School & RMIT School of Health Sciences

---

"Achieving and maintaining a happy and healthy lifestyle is a goal that many of us strive for, however integrating the changes required into our often busy and stressful lives can be difficult. In this book, Scott has suggested some simple changes we need to make to achieve our goal. Scott has summarised the evidence from a broad spectrum of scientific disciplines to provide the reader with an easy to follow guide to help us all achieve a happy and healthier life. Whilst this book is for everyone it, is of particular value to those suffering from chronic pain and disability who find themselves stuck in the negative cycle of helplessness."

Ian Cooper – Head of Department, Physiotherapy, Sir Charles Gairdner Hospital (SCGH)

"The world could greatly benefit from more health professionals like Scott! He clearly explains to his readers how not only exercise and nutrition, but thinking and emotions significantly affect the way our bodies feel and perform. Brilliant!"

Angi Covington – Brainwave Technologist and Author of 7 *Course Meal for the Soul – An Overview of the World's Greatest Teachings on Ultimate Happiness*

"Healthy, happy people are critical to well-connected and inclusive communities. One can't exist without the other. That's why I love this book. It's not just a guide but a fantastic kick start for people who want to turn around their mindset to achieving a healthy lifestyle – and make real change not only in their lives but those around them!"

John Carey – Mayor of Vincent, WA

"Scott provides a realistic marriage between medical and holistic approaches in a guide to ultimate happiness. This is a very readable and easy to follow approach to a healthy and happy life."

Tom Shieh –Speaker & Bestselling Author of *Boom!*

"As the CEO of The THRIVE Network, which assists people with intellectual and developmental disabilities live with dignity, respect and independence, I witness first hand the strength of the human spirit that allows EVERYBODY the chance to transform what can be known as debilitating moments into life-changing opportunities. Wescombe has captured that spirit in his latest book. The Wescombe Method builds connection and consensus with self, family, friends and other relationships."

Charles A. Archer – Attorney, Lecturer, Researcher and Bestselling Author of *Everybody Paddles: A Leaders Blueprint for Creating A Unified Team*

"Scott is a master at enhancing the quality of life of the people he serves. His passion, dedication and attention to service cause him to excel and puts him leagues ahead in his industry. The term 'go the extra mile' seems to be the phrase he lives by."

Roberta Brunin – Speaker, Coach & Author of *The Easiest Way To Get The Butt Out*

From Pain & Injury

To Healthy & Happy

GLOBAL PUBLISHING GROUP

Global Publishing Group
Australia • New Zealand • Singapore • America • London

From Pain & Injury To Healthy & Happy

SCOTT WESCOMBE

DISCLAIMER

All the information, techniques, skills and concepts contained within this publication are of the nature of general comment only and are not in any way recommended as individual advice. The intent is to offer a variety of information to provide a wider range of choices now and in the future, recognising that we all have widely diverse circumstances and viewpoints. Should any reader choose to make use of the information contained herein, this is their decision, and the contributors (and their companies), authors and publishers do not assume any responsibilities whatsoever under any condition or circumstances. It is recommended that the reader obtain their own independent advice.

Third Edition 2019

National Library of Australia
Cataloguing-in-Publication entry:

Creator: Wescombe, Scott J. (Scott Joseph), 1984- author.

From Pain & Injury to Healthy & Happy : Using the Breakthrough "Wescombe Method" / Scott Wescombe

2nd ed.
ISBN: 9781925288117 (paperback)

Mind and body therapies.
Therapeutics, Suggestive.
Psychophysiology.
Self-care, Health.

Dewey Number: 615.851

Published by Global Publishing Group
PO Box 517 Mt Evelyn, Victoria 3796 Australia
Email info@GlobalPublishingGroup.com.au

For further information about orders:
Phone: +61 3 9726 4133 or Fax +61 3 8648 6871

I dedicate this book to my amazing Mum & Dad who have been the greatest role models in my life, to my beautiful wife Tarryn who is the ultimate gift in my life, and finally to my siblings Luke, Joel and Lisa who have supported me since birth.

Scott Wescombe

Acknowledgements

It has been an honour and privilege to write this book. As with any major project, there are a number of very special people who contributed to making this book happen. So, I'd like to take this opportunity to say "THANK YOU".

Firstly, I am really grateful for the happy memories of my Nan, who was the primary inspiration for this book.

I would like to thank all of my friends, colleagues and teachers at both Edith Cowan University and Curtin University who shared insights, distinctions, methods, laughs and breakthroughs. A special thank you to Geoff Strauss, Ian Cooper and Amanda Mulcahy for their guidance and mentoring throughout my honours research project. I am also extremely grateful for the Subiaco Football Club for getting me to Perth and providing the opportunity to learn from Peter German, Matty Barber and the senior playing group – I walked away with a success formula for every aspect of life.

A special thank you to my Mum & Dad, Dianne & Gary; and brothers & sister, Luke, Joel, & Lisa; and my Grandparents for their utmost love and encouragement.

I also feel a deep sense of gratitude to:

- my Best Body family – for your relentless and passionate commitment to serving people in our communities with the latest and best treatment methods – you rock!
- the Best Body community – we have the best clients on this planet. It has been a privilege to serve, support and guide you!
- Daniel Webb and the Loftus Recreation Centre, team for your ongoing support and partnership and
- my dear friends and colleagues for your awesomeness.

A huge thank you to my publisher Global Publishing Group and their remarkable team, for your dedication and commitment to the book's success.

And finally, I thank my incredible wife Tarryn, who is my ultimate source of love, inspiration and courage on my mission to positively impact more people's lives. I am exceptionally grateful for your belief and faith in everything that I do and for your smile during the challenging moments. You mean the world to me!

FREE BONUS GIFT

(Valued at $150)

Claim your free bonus gift by going to

www.BestBody.com.au/bookbonus

The Wescombe Method 42-Day Kick Starters Guide

It includes:

- Simple and proven week-by-week guidelines to follow for nutrition, stress obliteration, sleep and exercise
- Essential information for monitoring your behaviour, thoughts and emotions
- How to get superior sleep for further energy to create better health and happiness
- The key principles of good nutrition that will boost the quality of your life
- The first steps on how to become a master of obliterating stress to avoid disease and maximise health
- Scientifically proven steps to unlock new levels of happiness

Contents

Introduction

I had just started studying physiotherapy at Curtin University and I was gearing up for a challenge. Everyone had told me that the degree would demand everything that I had. During the first week of University I got the devastating news that my beautiful grandmother, Nan as I called her, had passed away from cancer. I was devastated at not being able to travel from Western Australia to Tasmania for her funeral. Out of respect for my Nan, I committed more passionately than ever to always make her proud through the decisions I made as my career as a health professional developed.

Interestingly, I felt as if Nan was always watching over me as my career developed. As I progressed through my physiotherapy degree (my second degree), particularly towards the end, I started to realise how reactive the medical profession was. On my placements in the major hospitals, I saw that about 75% of the patients had preventable problems or diseases. Each time I experienced the impact that these preventable diseases had on the patient's family, it reminded me of my Nan's own death.

I grew up in a very small town, Cooee, in Tasmania and our house was about 200 metres from my grandparent's house. So my Nan had a strong influence on the person I am today; she was very intelligent, warm, loving and caring. Over the years I spent with her, she would always go straight to a medical or allied health professional as soon as something didn't feel right. She had many visits. She didn't smoke, drink alcohol and would rarely eat junk food. But she was very sedentary; she loved reading books, writing letters, knitting or other handcrafting and watching television.

I saw her slowly physically decline. It's not difficult for me now to understand why she developed colon cancer and then developed lung cancer, which eventually got the better of her. Even though it is only over recent years that the research has shown sedentary behaviour to be even unhealthier than smoking, the benefits of exercise for quality of life have been known for some time. Research on how sedentary behaviour increases the risk of certain cancers, including colon and lung cancers, suggested to me that the lack of physical daily activities and active behaviours may have contributed to Nan's cancers.

Initially, I was extremely frustrated that none of Nan's allied health or medical professionals did not see or explore the opportunities she had for better health and wellness, for example, living a more active lifestyle and strengthening and conditioning her physical body. The only thing that all of these professionals would ever do was focus on and treat the symptoms with tablets or 'Band-Aid' treatments.

It reminds me of a story I once heard from a doctor. There were 100 people who all drank from a water well and 97 of them suffered from gastrointestinal illness and all went to the local doctor, who prescribed antibiotics to every single person. Within a week, they were all better. A few days later, the same 97 people went back to the same doctor with the same symptoms after drinking from the water well again. The doctor once again prescribed antibiotics. The missed opportunity was the failure to test the water to get to the real cause of the problem. A lot of medicine is like that, giving antibiotics endlessly rather than checking the water.

After initially being extremely frustrated with all of the health and medical professionals, I appreciated that they all did the best they could do after being trained in medical school to think that way; to treat the symptoms rather than the causes, to focus on symptoms rather than people.

It seemed possible to me that if just one of the many health and medical professionals that consulted with my Nan had not only a conversation with her about exercise and lifestyle but also had kept her accountable for making positive changes in her life – to be pro-active versus re-active – she may still be with us today – and my mum would be a much happier person. Nan was a smart lady and would always follow the professionals' advice, and I believe she would have made the effort to make lifestyle changes that could have extended her life.

After witnessing the impact that the passing of my Nan had on my mother (they were best friends), I started to appreciate the importance of relationships to an individual's health and wellbeing. I promised myself that I would always understand an individual's relationship dynamics when serving them as a health professional, acknowledging that the person is a daughter, mother, wife, sister, cousin, neighbour and important to many people. I determined that I would always look at the opportunities the individual has to maximise their health, happiness and longevity. In other words, I vowed to have the conversation with my clients that I would have appreciated someone having with my Nan.

As I developed this philosophy, and while on student placements in hospitals, it became increasingly frustrating for me knowing that if I had of met the patient 5, 10, 15, or 20 years ago, he or she might not have been laying in that hospital bed surrounded by sad and grieving family and friends. These patients also would have enjoyed a much better quality of life following meeting me – which is priceless. That became a core value of mine – to enhance the life of every client that I meet.

This passion led me to open a physiotherapy practice straight out of university, so I could offer and deliver a service that I wholeheartedly believed in. There were no pro-active services in Perth at the time I started my first practice. Still today, many traditional health professionals do not know better, they purely treat the symptoms with interventions that have little or no evidence to support them, which ultimately means someone's Nan, sister, wife, daughter, brother, cousin may not be receiving the level of care they deserve or need.

Apart from my Nan, I have had other personal experiences that have taught me much about lifestyle and other factors that influence health and happiness. As a teenager I worked at two well known fast food outlets, and let me tell you that both of these places are great internships for up-and-coming health professionals. I used to eat pizza for breakfast and a lot of my food came from these establishments. Not surprisingly, I couldn't focus at school and struggled to stay awake, let alone be attentive. I dropped out of college after failing Year 11. I know first hand the huge impact of poor nutrition on mood, thoughts and behaviour and the amazing differences that occur when you work on optimising your lifestyle. Once I switched from multiple Cokes a day to water, from pizza, junk food, chocolate and ice-creams to nutritious food, my body developed and my focus skyrocketed. It completely changed my life.

Fortunately, I grew up in a sporting environment and watched my father coaching sprinters for many years. Even though I had poor lifestyle behaviours during certain stages of my childhood, I excelled at sports. While still in primary school, I broke multiple state records in athletics. I played Men's basketball as a teenager. I played football with the Subiaco Football Club in the WAFL and for Tasmania at the AFL National Under-18 championships. Over the past decade, I have talked to athletes and thousands of other people about the impact of a healthy lifestyle on peak performance from a position of valuable experience.

Another pivotal experience occurred during my University career. While the lessons above were about the enormous value of lifestyle on health, this lesson was about the role of mindset.

While I was at University I had the bright idea of day-trading using a loan from the bank! When the GFC hit, I lost it all, and it was a lot of money, at least for a student. I was angry with myself, ashamed and panicked. How was I going to repay the loan? I sank into a greater and greater depressive mindset, which wasn't helped by a trip to Bali with my best mate where – well, let's just say that I drank a lot. I was seriously thinking of dropping out of University. I couldn't focus and I was preoccupied with negative thoughts. Then I was placed on a spinal unit at a major hospital in Perth.

Many of the patients on this unit with significant spinal injuries had lost limbs, and most would never walk again. They were going to be completely dependent on others for the rest of their lives. The resilience shown by most of these patients was incredible. Despite the most horrendous circumstances, many of these paraplegic and wheelchair bound patients had an incredible attitude and a tremendous sense of inner peace. Their perseverance, dedication, internal motivation, drive and optimism following a major life challenge really touched me. It gave me new insights and perspectives on life as a whole, in terms of what is really important.

Firstly, I realised the quality of our life is directly related to our emotional home and how we choose to respond to each challenge life presents us. I saw firsthand, almost every day, how the best outcome will only be achieved through discovering the greatest meaning of the challenge. Resilience is the key to success.

The placement also completely changed the relationship I had with money. Inspired by the amazing human beings I was privileged to serve on that unit, I too vowed to find the opportunities in my life, to maximise what I can, both physically and emotionally. I discovered I could be healthy and happy regardless of my extremely poor financial situation – that red numbers did not limit my life – only negative thoughts could limit the quality of my life. I will be forever grateful for the unique experience I was gifted with during this time.

The experience also created a burning desire for me to serve people in the best way possible, and added to my motivation to create a private physiotherapy and fitness service of excellence that would help people experience life at a more effective and meaningful level. Ultimately, my goal is to raise the standard of living for as many people as possible, particularly through gaining better health, happiness and inner peace.

The principles that I cover in this book have been applied across thousands of clients in the physiotherapy and fitness clinics that I own and operate from. People just like you have discovered that pain is NOT normal, and that if they take the right steps and follow the right advice they too, can live a pain free life and move towards their best health and happiness.

My goal in writing this book is to show you – how you TOO – can move from Pain & Injury to Healthy & Happy.

I genuinely hope this book will achieve that goal for you.

If it is okay with you, I am going to offer you some coaching over the next couple of pages to truly enrich our journey together and boost your success in life from reading this book – my heartfelt gift to you.

Passive learning won't do – you can't just read this book and expect it to fix your back pain, headaches, or problems. You actually have to take the steps to implement what I guide you to do.

In short get your bum off that couch, do the exercises, modify your diet, change your thinking – MAKE IT HAPPEN!

#RaiseYourStandards

Books don't create change on their own, actions taken from thoughts created by books create change. The entire goal of this book is to plant thoughts in your mind which are healthy, which guide you out of pain, and which empower you with knowledge to make the right choices.

The problem is, though, this book can't make the choice for you. You are you and only you can make the decisions you need to make to live a pain free life. You must take responsibility for your current state of life, and through taking responsibility make a decision that there is a better way of living.

This is the VERY first decision that you must make. This book, any book, CANNOT help you to make that decision. What I write are just words on a page meant to inspire, motivate and educate you. What you do with that inspiration, motivation and education is up to you.

Think about it like this. When you went to school, you sat in a class of 20 to 30 people and each and every one of those people got the exact same education, in the exact same classroom, from the exact same teacher.

Some people embraced this education, asked questions, completed homework on time and studied outside of school hours, while others just cruised through. The ones that cruised through are probably lower on the career ladder right now then those who studied hard.

Now is your opportunity to study hard, now is your opportunity to do your homework, now is your opportunity to study outside of just this book. You really have to want to change. You need to want to live a healthy & happy life and be willing to take all and any actions necessary to achieve that goal.

The problem is, though, overtime people start to think it's normal and okay to live with pain. Some people even think it's part of the ageing process. The reality is so different to this thought pattern.

A healthy body does not trigger pain, a healthy mind does not trigger pain, and healthy eating and exercise habits can help prolong the period of healthy and happy living.

I'm not talking about 'new age' holistic approaches, I'm talking about the combination of KNOWLEDGE + ACTION + SUPPORT to achieve your goal of living healthier and happier.

Two of these things I am going to give you.

I am going to empower you with the KNOWLEDGE you need to

live a healthier and happier life. Not only that but I am also going to provide you the SUPPORT you need ongoing to ensure you take the RIGHT ACTION.

Understand though that ACTION is *your* responsibility. You are the one that needs to take action. I can provide you with all the knowledge and support you need, but without action it will be useless.

It would be like reading a Weight Loss book while eating a hamburger at a fast food outlet. Sure, the intention of reading a Weight Loss book was a great intention, but the actual execution of eating a fatty fast food hamburger while reading it means the person is not taking ACTION.

One thing may come as a surprise to you, as this wasn't something I discussed earlier. But as I am 100% committed to you living a healthier and happier life, I am providing you with SUPPORT beyond this book.

The support I am going to give is in the form of social support, multimedia support and ongoing digital support. It would also be an honour and privilege for me to be able to serve you in person one day soon hopefully.

The support is available to you online with a community of like-minded people. You can ask questions, meet new like-minded people, share your deepest and darkest thoughts. You can feel like you are in a happy, loving environment where all people accept you and know what you are working towards.

Combine that with added value, extra tips, ongoing support and you have the complete package you need to succeed.

Start Your Digital Journey To A Healthy & Happy Life At: www.BestBody.com.au/bookbonus

The big question that remains now is – what are you really trying to achieve and why? In the simplest form this book really has only one focus. While we talk about other principles and ideas, the key focus is empowering you to live a happy and fulfilled life.

Take this entire book as a complete lesson. Don't just read the first chapter and stop. Each chapter builds on the next and weaves a principle of living life.

Living sub-optimally not only affects the quality of your life. If you are suffering and are not so happy – how do you think that would make your family and friends feel? My guess – not so happy either. If you make a decision right now to step up and raise your standards of living to eliminate pain, and to live life at a level that you are capable of – how would you feel? How would it make your family and friends feel to see you making positive progress? You would be an inspiration.

Now is the time for you to realise that you can live not just a pain free life, but also a healthy & happy life. Go on, take the first step and make the decision that you deserve to live an extraordinary life!

Chapter 1

The Evolution of Medicine

Chapter 1

The Evolution of Medicine

"Medicine is not only a science: it is also an art. It does not consist of compounding pills and plasters. It deals with the very processes of life, which must be understood before they may be guided."

– Paracelsus

Let's start with a little bit of history. In the Western world, the concepts of art, religion and science co-existed well from at least the time of the Romans and the Greeks and even up to the early Renaissance in the fifteenth century. For example, Leonardo da Vinci was equally at home proposing scientific ideas as he was creating magnificent artworks. Even from classic times, the great thinkers like Aristotle preached about the marriage of art and science. However, by the seventeenth century the scientific method, as outlined by the famous French philosopher Descartes in his *Discourse on Method,* had become more defined. And this created a division that has dogged both Western science and medicine ever since.

Science and God

The context of the debate about what constituted 'real science' was the argument between scientists and the church, the dominant thought-leader at the time. As often happens, a deal was struck that was a function of the context rather than the truth: science claimed all that was observable, and the church kept all that was unobservable. Facts and faith were divided and, in a great example of human cognitive bias, the two philosophies became more and more polarised over time.

Let me introduce you to the notion of cognitive bias. Despite the fact that we human beings like to think we are logical, in many ways we are not. There has been a lot of cognitive neuroscience research over the past four decades and it has illuminated how we really think. The best book for a great summary of this research and its implications is by psychologist Daniel Kahneman and is called *Thinking, Fast and Slow.* Kahneman actually won the Nobel Prize for economics for showing that the idea of a rational economic man, which had endured for decades, was flawed, because people aren't logical. This has led to the revolution of *behavioural economics.*

For various reasons our brains like to keep things simple. We naturally categorise the world into black and white, when in reality it is infinite shades of grey. Studies in cognitive neuroscience show that we have inbuilt biases designed to make our thinking and decision making easier, rather than, necessarily, correct. Numerous studies show that we tend to categorise simplistically, have a very difficult time giving relative values to different concepts, and are very risk averse, to name three of the dozens of biases that have been identified.

The Halo Effect, for instance, refers to the fact that when someone is respected for one characteristic, e.g. their success, we overgeneralise this to other attributes, and overvalue the person.

The binary effect means that we tend to see things as either/or, rather than seeing the greater complexity that resides in almost every issue.

What this meant for the new world of science and medicine was that if you couldn't measure something, it wasn't important. Note the logical fallacy here – if scientists accepted that the immeasurable was important, then the divide between science and religion, fact and faith, becomes blurred once again. Objectivity was the essence of science, and anything that was subjective or that couldn't become measurable, was ignored, or at the very least undervalued. It was, and still is, hard to put a number to faith, belief, and even happiness. This has led to an almost slavish adherence to, and dependence on, so-called 'hard' data. This is particularly true in behavioural science. A survey of, for example, people's eating habits is conducted and the data treated as if it is gospel. However, people's recall of their eating habits is notoriously poor, so the data might be very unreliable to the point of being meaningless. But, because the data is in the form of numbers that can be the subject to logical analysis, the assumption is that the data is valuable, which in many cases is questionable.

Although we have come a long way from the days of Descartes, in some ways the underlying assumptions about 'objectivity' still remain in both science and medicine. As mentioned above, there is still a fixation on quantification and numbers, as if numbers by themselves are the truth. We can also be dazzled by technology. For example, functional Magnetic Resonance Imaging (fMRI) technology has been hailed as a window on the mind. By looking at blood-flow we can tell which areas of the brain are activated during different tasks and even during different moods. Certainly, the technology holds promise but its measurement is complex, and not as precise as it sounds. For example, one study showed that when photos of human beings in different emotional states were shown to a dead salmon, areas of the fish's brain were stimulated resulting in an fMRI response!

Measurement and hard data are, of course, still important but they can often be overvalued and other forms of information, like case studies and anecdotal evidence undervalued. Fortunately, technology and creativity have conspired to allow us to begin to measure previously abstract concepts and identify such things as the material infrastructure of emotions and other human characteristics, which have, up to now, been considered outside the reach of science. And they are showing that emotions and our mental life in general have a huge impact on our health.

Holistic versus Symptomatic Treatment

In the Orient, the Eastern tradition did not pit science against religion. Indeed spirituality has always been integrated into the oriental view of medicine and thus it has not been sidetracked by the artificial distinction embraced by the European Renaissance. As a result, today many principles of oriental medicine have been imported into the mainstream of western health and wellness; yoga and meditation in particular.

Because the oriental view of science grew out of a different tradition from Western science, oriental health practitioners focused on providing health rather than treating illness. The oriental holistic view considered the person, not microbes, bacteria, parasites and viruses, as the centre of health. The holistic tradition looks at the total interaction of the person with their environment, rather than separating the two into distinct parts. It has taken Western medicine a long time to catch up, and even today the false division still exists between the person and the physical environment in much of Western medicine. The Wescombe Method combines the best from both Eastern and Western medicine.

The Distinction Between Acute and Chronic Illness

The Western scientific and medical tradition was maintained, initially at least, by having many acute illnesses, and even conditions caused by nutrient deficiencies, to deal with. For example, in the 1740s scurvy ravaged the dominant British Navy, killing many more sailors than any human enemy. On long voyages, a fleet of British ships could lose as much as 70% of its men to the disease. When a Navy surgeon discovered that the problem was a lack of fresh fruits and vegetables, and more specifically the Vitamin C within, the problem was solved. Smallpox, polio and other acute conditions reinforced the notion that medicine was about treating the symptoms of the disease and then finding ways to eradicate the disease itself. The individual had no role to play in the course of the disease or its treatment.

Today, many of those previously devastating acute diseases have been eradicated or at least well controlled as a result of vaccinations and improved environmental conditions. Now, for the most part, the practice of medicine is not concerned with managing acute diseases but *chronic conditions* that are derived less by external factors and more by internal ones, including the patient's own actions, lifestyle and psychology. (*A popular definition from Wikipedia: Psychology simply refers to the study of the human mind and behaviour – including concepts such as perception, attention, emotion, motivation, personality, and interpersonal relationships to name a few.)*

Dealing with acute conditions, mentioned earlier, might have justified the 'scientific' approach but, of course, it didn't mean that other psychological factors, immeasurable at the time, weren't influencing the course of illness. In the Victorian era a famous physician, William Osler, wrote that he suspected that the response to treatment for tuberculosis, a rampant disease at the time, depended more on 'what the patient had in his mind than what he had in his chest.' This was an early recognition of the fact that even where there was an obvious physical pathology, psychology influences treatment response and recovery.

The answer is not an arbitrary distinction between the physical and the psychological, the seen and the unseen – it is about the interaction of both. By the late twentieth century, both scientists and technology had become more sophisticated, allowing for exploration of the interaction between pathogens (i.e. bugs) and people. However, a lot of medical practice today is still driven by the treatment of physical symptoms with scant consideration of the patient's feelings, thoughts and behaviour. One area where there has been a challenge to the orthodox medical treatment of potent medications, extensive imaging and expensive invasive surgeries is pain, specifically non-traumatic pain.

Ever since Freud, there has been the suggestion that some pain is either imagined or that 'real' pain is exaggerated by psychological factors. For the past generation New York physician Dr. John Sarno has continued this tradition by treating non-traumatic pain as a function of unconscious emotions, especially anger and rage.

According to Sarno, as expressed in his books like *The Divided Mind,* and *Healing Back Pain: A radical new approach to treating back pain,* non-traumatic pain is a coping mechanism to deflect the mind from dealing with emotional pain. The brain, Sarno argues, creates areas of reduced oxygen flow, stressing muscles, joints and tendons to create real pain, but the cause is psychological and not structural as the current medical practice implies. Sarno claims to have successfully treated thousands of people with this approach.

As you will read, there is a lot of behavioural research showing the connection between psychological factors such as mood and relationships to treatment response and general health. In addition, there is now evidence about *how* those factors, especially emotions, impact the body, making it more or less vulnerable to pain, injury, and disease. We need to move to a model that spends more time considering a person's opportunities and strengths rather than specific diseases. This is why I developed the breakthrough Wescombe Method.

Positive Psychology

In addition to the recognition that a person's mental state is inextricably bound up with their physical state – and the evidence that shows how this occurs – a third related development has come, in the form of positive psychology. This movement suggests that focusing on the positive rather than the negative or even the neutral, can have benefits for thought, action, behaviour and health. This school of thought suggests that health is more than the absence of disease, it is a dynamic positive state in its own right. Indeed positive psychology focuses on how people thrive and maximise their talents, rather than avoid getting sick. And this is a very important point...

Health is not just the absence of sickness. It is the active pursuit of joy, happiness and the maximal expression of skills and talents.

The Medical Experience

When you visit your doctor, does he or she spend any time exploring how happy you are, how fulfilled you are, and how much joy there is in your life? And if these issues are explored, are they discussed in terms of how you might put these in your life, or simply how stressed and depressed you might be because they are lacking?

If your doctor senses that things aren't going well in your life does he or she explore how it could be improved or just talk to you about prescribing an anti-depressant? Do they treat the symptom or address the issue? Do they talk to you about putting positivity in your life or do they prescribe a medication?

In a survey of Australian GP activity, the Australian Institute of Health and Welfare (AIHW, General Practice Activity in Australia 2009-10, Table 8.1: Summary of Management) found that prescriptions were recorded at rates of 83 per 100 encounters. A US survey from the Centre for Disease Control (CDC, National Ambulatory Medical Care Survey 2010, Tables 22,23,24) found that in 2010, 75% of doctor visits involved a prescription drug. Pain relievers, cholesterol lowering medications and anti-depressants were the most commonly prescribed. Another Centre for Disease Control survey (CDC, Health United States, 2014, Table 85) showed that between 2009 and 2012 almost half of Americans (48.7%) had used at least one prescription medication in the past thirty days and more than 10% had used five or more prescription drugs. These figures suggest that medications are at the centre of medical treatment at least in Australia and the USA. Even where modifiable lifestyle behaviours are responsible for medical conditions, we are still treating the symptoms with medications rather than addressing the lifestyle issues themselves.

There can be little doubt that stress plays a major role in health and has been implicated, not just in the recovery of illnesses like cancer, but also in their development in the first place. David Servan-Schreiber's book *Anti-cancer,* written by a man who is both a distinguished scientist and cancer sufferer, shows very clearly the relationship between cancer and lifestyle factors. As the author points out, all of us have cancer growing in us, but some of us have fully functional immune systems that prevent the cancer from developing, and others aren't so fortunate. And our mental states and lifestyles are the two most critical factors that determine how effective our immune systems are in fighting off diseases like cancer. If our mental states and behaviours influence our immune systems – critical in preventing or fostering illness and disease – then those states need to be the focus of medical attention if we really want to treat the cause rather than just the signs of illness.

The Focus of Treatment

I have already mentioned cognitive bias and I will continue to refer to it throughout the book. There's another way bias, and therefore perception, influences health and the practice of medicine.

Let me ask you a few questions. What is your relationship with your doctor like? Do you feel like a case number or does your doctor treat you like a real person? Is the conversation with your doctor an authentic one or superficial? Can you tell your doctor exactly what is on your mind, or do you keep the conversation to pleasantries? Is the conversation with your doctor limited to your symptoms or does it encompass your entire life?

If your relationship with your doctor or any health professional is such that your interaction with him or her is merely restricted to discussion of symptoms and potential treatment, then a visit won't be a very pleasant experience. It will focus on the negative and it might be associated with anxiety and concern.

If, on the other hand, your relationship with your doctor or any health professional is authentic, based on honesty and trust, and always encompasses your life and overall well being in relation to your health, then a visit will be a positive experience. The relationship and the conversation that follows from it will be meaningful and therefore have real value. The conversation won't just focus on what's wrong, but what's right, too. You will be able to see any symptoms you have in context of you as a person and your life in general, rather than isolated, external negatives that need to be treated. You will also be more likely to be completely engaged with any treatment suggestions – actually you will have been part of the decision-making process about exactly what 'treatment' is. In short, the visit will be about you as a whole person, and it will involve you. Rather than being told what to do, you will be an active participant in any treatment plan.

The authentic relationship with your health or medical professional will mean that *together* you will devise a plan that focuses on the development of positive behaviours that will not only impact your mental state and the symptoms you are experiencing but your overall quality of life. This is the model of care that I espouse and believe is essential to effective health or medical practice.

The remainder of the book explores all of the points I have mentioned above in more detail. I will provide evidence to show that focussing on strengths and on the whole person is far more effective than treating symptoms for several reasons. I will show you the amazing world of psycho-neuro-immunology (PNI), which reveals how emotions – and even the thoughts that can engender them – impact every cell in your body. I will show you why the quality of personal relationships are critical to your physical health. I will show you that health isn't about the absence of disease but about fulfillment and happiness. Let's continue our journey together.

"Medicine is the restoration of discordant elements; sickness is the discord of the elements infused into the body."

– Leonardo Da Vinci

Chapter 2

The Brain, Stress and Disease

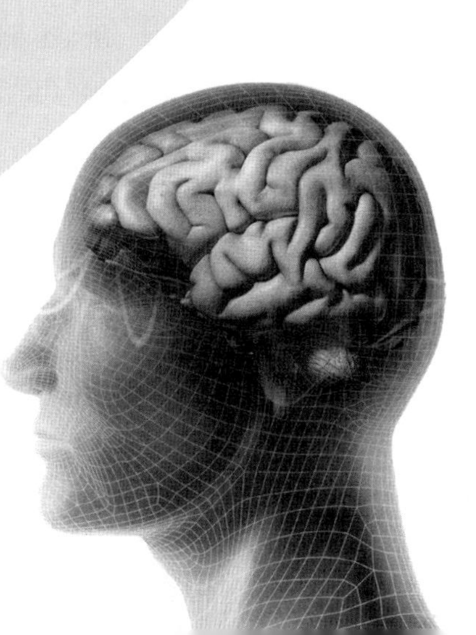

Chapter 2

The Brain, Stress and Disease

"It is more important to know what sort of person has a disease than to know what sort of disease a person has."

– Hippocrates

In the previous chapter I briefly reviewed the history of medicine and suggested that it is based on the notion that medical practice is designed to treat symptoms of illness, not causes, and has developed from a view in which patients were not considered responsible for acute diseases and illnesses. However, today most medical treatment deals with chronic problems that are often at least in part due to the individual's behaviour, and that is a reflection of the world in which we now live.

Today's major diseases are cardiovascular disease, diabetes, stroke, cancer and the dementias, the latter being expected to increase dramatically as the population ages. Dementias, including Alzheimer's Disease, was projected to cost the USA $226 billion in 2015, a figure which is expected to increase to $1.1 trillion by 2050. Even though there are some genetic contributions to each of these diseases, lifestyle behaviours seem to contribute a lot to the development of these conditions. Yes, there is growing evidence that nutrition influences the risk of Alzheimer's and dementia. Studies have shown that the Mediterranean Diet and, probably, a vegan diet reduce the risk of both dementia and Alzheimer's. Excess weight, poor nutrition, lack of physical activity, poor sleep patterns and high levels of stress combine to strain the body and make it vulnerable in many different ways.

These unhealthy lifestyle behaviours come in part from a response to the heavy demand and pace of modern society. We are consumed, literally and metaphorically, by the chase for material possessions. The distinction between work and rest has become ever more blurred as a result of technology that allows us to be connected and plugged in 24/7. Seeking a necessary balance in life, let alone peace and happiness, can be seen as a bad career move.

Our human brains weren't designed for this sort of overwhelming input and constant processing. They weren't really designed to pursue greater and greater workloads and more and more possessions. The human brain is best when it works with fundamental human needs rather than getting overwhelmed with human wants. Our brains have not adapted to the demands of modern society. However, as we shall see, the brain is very malleable and trainable and it continues to do what we humans train it to do.

The human brain is often divided into three distinct areas, reflecting different stages of evolutionary development. The 'reptilian' brain is responsible for fundamental physical processes like breathing. It is also responsible for the survival, fight-or-flight response. The second brain is the 'mammalian' brain (sometimes called the limbic brain) and it is responsible for feelings and memory. It links feelings with behaviour and can add a level of control over the reptilian brain's more instinctive responses. Both the reptilian and mammalian brain operate subconsciously and without a sense of time. Moreover, both of these systems can't detect real from imagined threat.

The 'neocortex', representing about 85% of the brain's volume, is the most recently evolved and allows us to use language, judge, think and plan – the executive function we need to control, plan and manage our behaviour.

These brain areas aren't disconnected and there are many interconnections that allow for integrated action. However, in difficult and emotion-laden situations the reptilian and mammalian brains are typically in control. Despite the fact that we humans think we are logical, reason only prevails in perhaps 20% of the time. When emotion, threat and even pleasure are involved, the reptilian and mammalian brains conspire to protect us and serve their needs. They draw on experiences and memories to subconsciously drive behaviour. The cortex cannot overcome these two powerful systems and under these conditions will offer up rationalisations to go along with the older brain's decisions. For example, even though your conscious intention is to reduce calories and avoid sweets because you want to lose some weight for an upcoming family event, when you see a delicious piece of chocolate cake that your older brain knows is pleasurable and will provide energy, your older brain will prevail, while your neocortex creates the rationalisation that 'this one piece won't hurt' or 'I've been good all day,' or some other elegant excuse.

So the older brain still controls many of our reactions. Specifically, survival is still the brain's main imperative and our reactions are still based on the idea that threat is a physical threat come to harm us or a predator come to eat us. As a result, the reptilian brain interprets threat as a physical threat and our stress response is geared to deal with predator lions and aggressive mammals. Our response to stress has not evolved beyond being chased in the savannah. It doesn't matter that today's stressors are often related to non-physical threats like debt and troubled relationships, we still react to everything as if we are about to be eaten.

When faced with any sort of threat, the stress response, or the appropriately named fight-flight syndrome, gears us up to run or fight. When stressed our brain prepares us for action. Adrenaline is pumped out. Blood goes away from the organs to galvanise muscles into action. A host of chemicals, from endorphins to cortisol, are produced that bring a cascade of changes in the endocrine and immune systems. Attention becomes narrowed as we focus on threat. Perception becomes attuned to the negative as we search for danger. The reptilian brain is not interested in happiness; it just wants to fight or run – and win. And we continue to follow where the reptilian brain leads us. The fight-flight system literally goes into action in milliseconds, not waiting to see if the threat that has been detected is real or not. That decision is left to the slower frontal cortex, which while the reptilian brain is directing our physical responses, is more deliberately determining the extent – and reality – of the threat. For example, if you're walking in the forest and out of the corner of your eye you see the outline of what looks like a snake, you will instinctively jump back or even run. In a second or so your frontal cortex has determined it's not a snake but a piece of rope. You breathe a sigh of relief but you have already started to sweat and your heart rate has rocketed – all in less than second.

The reptilian brain isn't really geared for chronic stress. It was designed to be capable of short bursts of activity, after which it focuses on conserving energy for the next run-in with a predator. The fight-flight response is adaptive and protective – in short spells. The physical response works well for getting in a fight but it doesn't do so well when you are constantly worrying about how you are going to pay your bills, or you are fretting over a work situation, or dealing with a break-up of a relationship. In these situations, the stress response doesn't work for two reasons. First, it is an inappropriate response as the dangers are not physical threats, and second, a prolonged stress response paradoxically produces life-threatening responses not life-saving ones.

The autonomic system, which orchestrates the stress response, is a great example of the misguided notion (and cognitive bias) that if a small amount of something is good for you, a lot of it must be better. Rather than benefitting from an overload of stress hormones, immune system activation and the like, a prolonged stress response starts to produce opposite effects. It's as if the body has thrown all its reinforcements into battle and as time passes there is nothing left to defend itself, leaving it vulnerable rather than protected.

In so many ways, prolonged stress – and the response it typically induces – is responsible for many of today's health and medical issues. Whether you are talking about the major chronic diseases outlined at the beginning of this chapter like heart disease and cancer, or whether you are talking about aches, pains and migraines, prolonged stress increases the probability of illness by reducing your body's ability to defend itself.

It used to be thought that stress was only responsible for heart disease and ulcers. Now we know it can make you vulnerable to almost anything by weakening the immune system. For example, the current view about cancer is that all of us have cancers growing in us but a healthy immune system can do its job and take care of the dangerous cells. But if your immune system is compromised, cancer cells can grow and develop into a major problem. The same model applies to many other conditions where the immune system loses its ability to effectively deal with antigens ('anti-gens' literally means 'not self') that are not part of the body, thus putting health at risk.

It's not just the impact of the stress response itself that is damaging. Compensatory behaviours that we adopt to manage our stress bring their own problems. As stresses and workloads impact our daily lives we find ways to boost our energy through unhealthy behaviours, especially eating.

The relatively new field of neuro-energetics is about how the brain gets its energy. The brain doesn't really store energy, so when it needs it – and it needs a lot when under stress – it typically goes in to the body to get it. Although the brain is 2% of body weight it uses about 25% of the body's energy stores. Those energy stores are mostly glucose, and the brain uses about 450 calories of glucose every day, more when stressed. However, in this mechanism, called the 'brain-pull', the brain increases the release of glucose by activating the stress system. This results in 'cerebral insulin suppression' (CIS) giving the brain more glucose. Interestingly, recent studies show that in some obese people, this mechanism doesn't work well and then an alternative strategy has to be found to fuel the brain. If you can't get the brain energy from within the body then the only alternative is to go outside the body – and that means going directly to the food source. So now you know why some people lose weight under stress and others gain it.

Society, in the form of successful businesses, has of course catered to our needs. Businesses that make it easy and convenient to satisfy our needs will thrive and over the past hundred years, there has been a burgeoning business literally catering to our energy needs. This has come in different forms; the rise of processed foods, fast food, coffee and the presence of sugar in almost everything.

A hundred years ago the annual consumption of sugar in the USA was just five pounds or 2.3kg a person. Today it is – wait for it – a staggering 190 pounds or 86.2kg of sugar! While fat is often portrayed as the main nutritional villain, the fact is that the evidence is mounting that sugar is the real poison. Admittedly, trans fats in the form of partially hydrogenated oils have been shown to be really damaging and are soon likely to be removed from the market place. But sugar is responsible not just for diabetes and weight related conditions, because it also stimulates inflammation and it is an influence on the development of cancer and dementia, to name but two major illnesses. So the cycle is that stress creates the need for more energy, which leads to a marketplace conveniently offering poor nutritional choices which compound our problems by making us more vulnerable.

Stress impacts our lifestyle in other ways. Despite the fact that one of the purposes of stress is to galvanise us into physical action, under stress people are less likely to exercise. In fact, when people are stressed it is common for them to stop exercising rather than making it more of a priority. Under chronic stress, sleep can also be compromised. Good quality sleep has important restorative functions and rejuvenates the mind and the body. Poor sleep deprives you of these important functions, rendering you just not fatigued and low in energy, but vulnerable. Of course, there are many ways in which all of these factors combine. Someone making poor nutritional choices gains weight. As a result of their weight gain they develop sleep apnea. As a result of the apnea, they have low energy and are mentally and physically compromised. The vicious cycle has started.

Other factors conspire to keep us locked in this self-defeating cycle. One of these is the concept of 'social proof.' Social psychologists and sociologists have shown quite categorically that a big influence on our behaviour is what we see other people doing. Working with monkeys, they found a system of 'mirror neurons' that seem to underpin the primate ability to relate to what others are doing. We are capable of experiencing empathy and compassion, and mirror neurons seem to be the hardware that mediates those feelings. We are therefore programmed to copy what we see going around us, and this makes the actions of others a big influence on behaviour. Simple examples of this include the contagiousness of a yawn, or copying people who are looking upwards at who-knows-what. All of this means that when, for example, 70% of population are overweight, it's easy to follow suit.

Another factor that keeps us locked in to unhealthy behaviour has to do with the brain itself. By and large the brain lives in the present. It discounts events that are more than a few weeks into the future and when the chips are down the older brain, working subconsciously and on past experiences prevails, leaving the cortex to make excuses. So while we know we should exercise, eat better, get quality sleep, unless we are suffering *right now,* the threat of future vulnerability is severely discounted. Without the emotional connection to consequences of behaviour that are prevalent in the present, it's easy to delay changing behaviour. Sure you might want to look good for that family event in six months time but the immediate pull of that chocolate cake is far stronger than some conceptual event in the future.

Social proof, future discounting and the subconscious processing of our older brain make it difficult for people to change habits and behaviours. The success rate for changing ingrained and constant habits, like diet, smoking and even addictions, is generally notoriously poor with long-term success rates as low as 10%. It's illustrative that the success rates are very similar no matter what habit is targeted for change suggesting that it is the general nature of habit rather than any specific habit, which makes change so difficult. However, using the Wescombe Method when working with thousands of clients one on one, I have enjoyed extraordinarily high success rates – and I am extremely grateful to have had the privilege of serving those individuals, families, and sports teams.

Another reason why habits in general are difficult to change is the regularity of the behaviour. The *constancy* of behaviour is critical. For example, eating three times a day every day is not just a constant exposure to food but is reinforcing the brain, subconsciously racking up thousands of associations, and training it to adapt to this exposure. Consider smoking, where a heavy smoker is training his or her brain and body to expect nicotine and the other chemicals in smoke about 200 times a day (ten puffs on 20 cigarettes). That's a very heavy reinforcement schedule. Not only will such a pattern make it difficult to quit because of withdrawal, the behaviour and the physiological impact of smoking will be ingrained in the brain and body. There will be numerous conscious and subconscious associations with other internal (e.g. mood) and environmental (e.g. place) cues that can restore the behaviour at a moment's notice, even after weeks of a new behaviour of limited indulgence or even abstinence. Relapse is a real issue in all forms of behaviour change, a testimony to the power of associations formed over years of repetition and exposure. This constancy of behaviour is a powerful contributor to the creation of habit. While it makes changing behaviour hard, it also gives us clues about how to develop healthier habits and I will talk about this more in a later section.

As a result of all of these factors we are faced with an epidemic of stress-induced problems. The answer has been to try to fix the fallout from the reptilian brain's stress response, and focus on changing negative behaviours.

But there's an alternative to this approach.

In the last decade we have learned a lot about the ability to change the brain in significant ways. Many studies have shown that the process of neuroplasticity is a critical and lifelong process during which the brain adapts to situations, some of which are consciously intended. This opens the possibility that instead of accepting the reptilian and mammalian brain's control over our behaviour, we make the effort to more consciously control them. There's the real chance that we can develop our strengths so we can control emotions and the stress response, rather than have them control us. The recognition that we can change our brains through conscious effort is an amazing step forward in changing our perception about health and wellness. In the next chapter I will explore the mind-blowing world of neuroplasticity.

"The aim of medicine is to prevent disease and prolong life. The ideal of medicine is to eliminate the need for a physician."

– William Mayo

Chapter 3

Neuroplasticity

Chapter 3

Neuroplasticity

"Our minds influence the key activity of the brain which then influences everything; perception, cognition, thoughts and feelings, personal relationships; they're all a projection of you."

– Deepak Chopra

I hope you have enjoyed our journey together so far – I am gratified you have chosen this pathway. This chapter is fascinating!

The brain is an incredible organ. It consists of about a hundred billion cells each capable of thousands of connections. The cells themselves are incredible works of nature, producing changes in electrical potential that send messages through the dendrites (cell branches) to other neurons. These networks of interconnections that send messages up and down the brain, from the older reptilian brain to the newer neocortex, and across the brain from the frontal lobes to the back of the brain, are the key to how we think, feel, react and behave.

Until fairly recently, it was generally assumed that cell growth and adaptation was limited to the early years of life. It was apparent that childhood, through the early stages of adulthood into about the late twenties, was the times of greatest learning. In childhood, there are the potential networks consisting of millions of neural connections and networks. In adolescence, there is some pruning of these networks that begins to limit the potential. As a result, behavioural change and adaptation seemed to be more difficult and less possible the older we get. It used to be thought that the forties were the upper age limit for such adaptation and that after that age, positive brain change wasn't possible. We know that the frontal cortex, responsible for thinking, judgment, planning and other executive functions, isn't fully developed until the late twenties, suggesting that there is natural adaptation and change through at least that stage of life. However, recent research has shown that while growth and learning are indeed maximised early in life, that networks are indeed pruned in adolescence, the ability to adapt and change is a possibility throughout the lifespan. You really can teach an old dog new tricks and sometimes those new tricks can significantly alter brain function and even brain structure, leading to new behaviours and, potentially at least, greater control over behaviour, and improved happiness and wellbeing that can change health as well as outlook. Neuroplasticity research suggests that there can be changes to nerve cells, changes in the interconnection of cells leading to new pathways, and the development of new cells. All of these can reflect major changes to how we perceive and act in the world around us.

Cortical Maps

It has been known for a long while that different brain functions, especially functions involving muscles, sensory input and motor movement, were associated with different parts of the brain. A map, called a homunculus (literally 'a small man') was adopted by scientists to represent where different functions were located in the brain. It should be said that the brain is an integrated organ that uses the interconnectivity of different parts to operate effectively. Nonetheless, it appeared to early neurologists that areas of the brain 'housed' specific functions. This mapping allowed for the possibility of what happened to the cortical map in the event of trauma and injury. Would the map change in any way in the event of pain, injury, trauma and disease?

The rearrangement of cortical maps was initially observed in people who had traumatic brain injuries and amputations. When an area of the brain was damaged it appeared that functions associated with it could be relocated to nearby areas of the brain, especially if the damaged limbs and parts of the body were utilised, and even exercised through activities like physical rehabilitation. Some of the early research showed, for example, that when an animal suffered an amputation of a digit, the neighboring digits became associated with that area of the brain that had 'housed' the amputated one. So physical functions could take over associated brain locations. The reverse has also been found to be true, brain locations can take over physical functions. This is the reason for 'phantom limbs' which occur when people who have had limbs amputated still feel the presence of the limb. This actually occurs in a majority of amputees and is a result of the region of the brain formerly associated with the amputated limb being stimulated by an adjacent area of the body. The cortical map changes and adapts to circumstances.

Another demonstration of the relocation of function came in a study on adult squirrel monkeys that had lesions that affected their hand movements. Retraining the animals had the effect of changing their cortical maps. In some instances, hand movements were now associated with areas on the cortical map that were previously associated with shoulder and elbow movements. Similarly, a study investigating stroke victims, showed that using the hand that had been most affected by the stroke led to greater changes in blood flow in several areas of the brain compared to those who never had a stroke. Hand movements were now associated with different areas of the brain.

The above research has been reflected by, and reinforced in, clinical cases where there have been brain injuries like stroke or traumatic injury. Subsequent changes to the 'cortical map' have been seen, again suggesting that the brain has the capacity to relocate motor functions from a damaged area to a non-damaged one. However, such relearning and cortical map reorganisation probably depends on other critical areas of the brain functioning normally. For example, damage to the hippocampus, the area of the brain implicated in memory, significantly reduced rats' recovery of function after injury, suggesting that cortical reorganisation and thus plasticity depend on functional memory and learning structures.

In addition to the rearrangement of cortical maps, the development of new interconnections and pathways represent another significant way our brains can be changed by experience.

On Monkeys, Rats and Musicians

There have been numerous studies with animals and humans that demonstrate that experience can rearrange the brain's connections, resulting in new learning. In one study, two groups of monkeys were divided on the ease in which they could acquire food. One group had it easy – they were given the food. Another group had to search for it and then use complex motor movements to free the food from where it was stored. On examination at the end of the experiment, the latter group had increased their brain topography developing new areas in the motor cortex, presumably a result of their learning how to become more dextrous. In similar studies, rodents learning a skilled motor task showed more development in the motor areas of the brain than those doing a less skilled task.

Such changes have also been shown in humans, too. A study with musicians also struck the right chord and showed results that were in harmony with animal studies. One study showed musicians who played stringed instruments had more developed areas of the brain associated with fine motor movement of the hand than musicians who didn't play stringed instruments. Another study compared the brain's response to tones in non-musicians, amateur, and professional musicians. The data showed that the level of musical sophistication was associated with an increased amount of grey matter in the relevant brain area. The obvious and reasonable assumption is that practice develops these brain areas. It's possible, however, that the observed differences reflect natural structural differences that have always been there. Some people might have a brain structure and function that predisposes them to manifest musical talent. Another study, again with musicians, addressed the issue of whether observed brain changes were innate or learned.

In this noted study, professional keyboardists were compared to amateurs and non-musicians. Not only did the professionals have more grey matter in various skill-related areas of the brain suggesting that new connections had been formed, but the key finding was the increased grey matter volume was associated with the *amount of time spent practicing*, strongly suggesting that the brain changes were a function of learning. If the brain can be rewired through injury and circumstance can we consciously change the brain with deliberate action?

Meditation

There has been a lot of recent buzz about the impact of the meditation on the brain. There have been numerous reports of meditation positively impacting the brain, but caution is required here. There are many types of meditation and a lot of the research has used different variations, so it can be difficult to generalise findings. Much of the research has also used very small numbers, again making the generalisability of findings difficult. Also, many works refer to the brains of people such as Buddhist monks who seem to be different than your typical first world inhabitant. Buddhist monks and other similar community members have very different lifestyles from the average Westerner. They live in spiritual communities and are free from many of the anxieties and stresses of modern man or woman.

So any observed differences might be due to lifestyle factors other than meditation. Nonetheless, there is good reason to believe that meditative practices can have a significant impact on the brain.

Often in meditation studies, more experienced practitioners are compared to less experienced counterparts and typically the more experienced and practiced meditators show more pronounced brain changes. As we age, the thickness of the cortex is reduced and this is associated with the diseases of ageing. In one study, experienced meditators showed less decline in cortical thickness and better performance on an attention test than others, suggesting that meditation may have some protective effects against the physical brain changes that accompany ageing. Whatever was responsible for the superior performance of these experienced meditators, whether it was lifestyle, spirituality, compassion, meditation or a combination of all of these factors, it is a great demonstration of how maximising potential can significantly impact the brain and overall health. If meditation, or any activity, really does have the ability to reduce or postpose dementia, it would be a major breakthrough, given the devastating financial and social cost of the disease, which is overwhelmingly huge and only, projected to get bigger.

In another study, meditators showed a decrease in the size of the amygdala, an important brain structure involved with the processing of stress and the fight-flight response. A reduction in the amygdala could translate into a greater ability to manage emotion, a very important consideration that is at the heart of the principle of this book; conscious management of stress and emotion. In terms of the brain hierarchy, neocortical control of the mammalian and reptilian brain would allow for better health and wellness by managing instinctive impulses, enhancing the immune system and the stress response.

In that same study, where the amygdala was reduced in volume in meditators, there was evidence that meditation was associated with an increase in the caudate, an area of the brain associated with the processing of uncomfortable emotions like sadness. Again, the reduction of 'negative' or difficult, uncomfortable emotions would confer a big health advantage as will be outlined in subsequent chapters.

Meditation typically involves Alpha and Theta brainwave activity, waves that are, not surprisingly, associated with relaxation, intuition and less information processing, characterised by increased Beta wave activity. In fact Mindfulness Based Stress Reduction (MBSR) was introduced by Jon Kabat-Zinn in the USA and has shown to be effective in reducing moods, stress and depression. It's possible that such activities like MBSR and even related activities like deep breathing and yoga, can help provide conscious control of emotional states, leading to enhanced wellbeing and health. There are suggestions from some studies that both meditation and MBSR increase compassion. The notion is that these techniques enhance empathy and connectedness.

Brain waves and associated states of consciousness

Delta waves	1-4 cps	sleep
Theta waves	4-8 cps	light sleep, deep relaxation
Alpha waves	8-13 cps	relaxed wakefulness
Beta waves	13-30 cps	processing, stress, rumination

Researchers know no geographical boundaries in their exploration of neuroplasticity. One famous study found an unlikely group of research subjects in London cabbies – or more precisely those trying to become London taxi cab drivers. If you have ever been to London you will have learned that there is neither rhyme nor reason to the way the streets are named and laid out. As a result, if you want to be a London cab driver, you have to literally memorise the names and locations of hundreds of streets and their relationship to each other. In fact, there are 25,000 streets within a few miles of a central spot in London, Charing Cross Station. Getting your cabbie license takes a long time; three or four years, and requires a lot of memorisation and learning.

Some enterprising neuroscience researchers capitalised on the learner London cabbies and looked at the effect of all this learning on the brain. Using brain imaging and cognitive tests, the researchers investigated the hippocampus, the main part of the brain involved in this sort of memorisation and learning. Not surprisingly perhaps, the researchers showed that the hippocampus of many of the student drivers grew over the course of their training. Growth seemed to be related to success, with the more proficient students showing more hippocampal growth than the less successful ones.

Echolocation

The possibilities of neuroplasticity are endless but there's one story that for me captures the promise of this approach for medicine, health and wellbeing. It is the story of an amazing guy called Daniel Kish.

At first glance you might not see anything unusual about Daniel Kish. He walks around, rides a bike, he does a lot of things that healthy people do. There's one difference, though. Daniel Kish is blind. He has been blind since the age of two. However, Daniel did something unusual. Instead of looking at his weakness, he developed a strength. Not just a strength but an amazing ability that perhaps no one in the history of mankind had ever developed.

For whatever reason, after he was blinded Daniel started to make clicking sounds with his tongue. Eventually using the echoes reflected back to him to locate objects in space, Daniel was able to navigate through the environment. He had taught himself echolocation. Echolocation is used by animals such as bats and dolphins for navigation and now Daniel had taught himself how to do it too. Typically, the visual areas of the brains of blind people become dormant. However, when scientists looked at Daniel Kish's brain they found new connections in the brain between his visual and auditory areas, which allowed Daniel to 'see' sounds. This wasn't just a one-off miracle. Daniel has taught this skill to hundreds of people. It is a wonderful example of what can happen when we develop our strengths rather than focusing on our weaknesses.

Neurogenesis

It has now been established that we can and do grow new brain cells throughout the lifespan. This process, called neurogenesis, allows new brain cells to replace nonfunctioning or dead ones. At this point new brain cells seem to be limited to certain areas of the brain, specifically the hippocampus, the hub that organises memory. It is not just the ability to grow new cells that is important, it is the ability to keep new cells alive and make them functional that is also crucial.

Certain activities seem to be associated with the ability to grow functional new brain cells. Not surprisingly, it appears that if new cells created by neurogenesis are going to survive, they need to be exercised. Exercise for new cells in the hippocampus means learning new information and even new skills. Physical movement also appears to be central to effective neurogenesis. In various studies aerobic exercise seemed to be an important variable in successful neurogenesis. Aerobic exercise in general has also been associated with better brain health, some research showing that regular aerobic activity was associated with less cortical atrophy and improved cognitive function.

There is, therefore, a lot of evidence that shows that the brain can be changed for the better by consciously directed activity. The brain will adapt to circumstances, which means if we focus on stress and difficulties we are likely to encourage disease and malfunction across all of our important biological systems. On the other hand, if we mindfully pursue positive activities, we can significantly improve our brain and thus our overall wellbeing for the better.

Our greatest human adventure is the evolution of consciousness. We are in this life to enlarge the soul, liberate the spirit, and light up the brain.

– Tom Robbins

Chapter 4

Thoughts

Chapter 4

Thoughts

"Thoughts can either supercharge or strangle every cell in our bodies – the magic is where we habitually choose to put our focus"

– Scott Wescombe

In the last chapter I showed how actions can change the brain in remarkable ways. However, the ability to influence the brain and its functions goes beyond actions; it includes our very own thoughts. Our thought processes as well as our thoughts themselves have a big influence on our brains as well as our bodies. It's not just that our thoughts influence and guide our actions and those actions impact the brain and our bodies, it is that thoughts on their own can produce powerful effects – for better or for worse. In this chapter, I will look at how thinking in its different forms impacts us much more than we might imagine. Are you ready to find out?

There was an interesting study conducted by Dr. John Bargh and his colleagues at New York University. In this research, college students were given the task of creating four word combinations from a list consisting of five words. The lists typically contained fairly neutral words. One list however had associations with ageing and consisted of the words 'Florida, gray, wrinkle, bald, forgetful'. The research subject students who were working on this list seemed to be affected in an unexpected and unconscious way. When these student subjects subsequently walked down a hallway, they did so significantly slower than those subjects who had not been exposed to words associated with ageing.

When the student subjects were told of the finding, they reported that they had no awareness that they were walking slowly and weren't mindful at all that they were influenced in any way by the words associated with ageing.

What is interesting about this study is the words weren't about ageing, they were merely *associated* with ageing. The list of words didn't include direct references to ageing like *dementia, Alzheimers, senility*, but words that were associated with it. This is important and says a lot about how the mind works. Sensory input of any kind can trigger associations based on experience and learning. I'm sure that certain songs, for example, evoke memories and associations in you, as do smells, sights, sounds and even tastes or feelings. This is all part of how the mind tries to make sense of the world.

If you find the above research findings mysterious, think about your own experience. If you have been having a wonderful, uplifting conversation with some one who is full of energy and hope, how do you feel when engaged in that interaction? If you are having a conversation with someone who is complaining about all the stresses in life and how difficult it is dealing with all of the obstacles and challenges, how do you feel when engaged in that interaction? We have the inbuilt unconscious ability to feel what others are feeling – the basis of empathy and compassion. Isn't it likely that you will be feeling good during an uplifting conversation and not feeling so good during a depressing one? And that power to turn on emotions by mere thought and association is an important part of the dynamic of how the mind can influence the body.

"We are blind to our blindness. We have little idea of how little we know. We're not designed to know how little we know."

– Daniel Kahneman

I have already mentioned the survival imperative that has the brain constantly searching for threats and seeking to deal with them by either activating the fight-flight response or conserving energy for when it has to go into action mode. But the brain also has a drive to make sense of the world; it has the need to organise its experience so that it can tell whether it's safe, predict when it might not be, and generally feel that it controls its environment. In order to do this it receives input from the world through sensory information and then has to organise the input in some coherent way, and then store that organised experience in memory. In short, it has to create a story about what is happening.

We receive sensory input and it has associations for us. This creates a perception of what is happening that is then put into memory as a story or narrative. This process is much more intuitive than logical and involves several leaps of association.

Philosophers and psychologists from William James to Sigmund Freud to contemporary thinkers like Bruce Mangan, distinguish between sensory information, like the colour and appearance of a bird, and non-sensory information, which is really abstract feelings about the sensory information, in this case, the sight of the bird. These non-sensory experiences have been called the "fringe of consciousness" and are thought to represent the massive set of unconscious associations that surround the sensory impression of the bird. These might include the name of the bird, feelings about the bird, and vague feelings about the situation in general. This fringe of consciousness has been compared to the toolbar of a word processing program. The bulk of the screen that occupies your attention is the document you are working on – the sensory impression. The toolbar represents the non-sensory fringe, which allows access to many features that can shape the document. This analogy is appealing in that the non-sensory fringe is assumed to have so many associations that they would overwhelm consciousness if they were all available, just like all the elements of the toolbar when fully exposed would overwhelm the screen and your document if they were the focus of attention.

This non-sensory fringe, contains unconscious associations that frame perception and determine the context of sensory impressions and even thoughts. In other words, how we interpret what we see, hear, smell, taste and touch, is heavily influenced by a fringe of a mass of vague associations that we can't effectively evaluate but produce strong feelings of familiarity and rightness – or the opposite. We experience this as 'gut feel' – a strong sense that we are on the right track (or not) which heavily influences our following thoughts, decisions and behaviour. What that means is that a big influence on our thoughts, opinions and decisions – possibly the decisive one – is not available for conscious, let alone rational, consideration.

Imagine you are walking down the road and, as a red SUV passes, you hear the sound of a car horn. Instantly you make the association that your friend Jack owns a red SUV and conclude (actually assume) that he has just acknowledged you by honking his horn. The thought of Jack ignites an association in your head; the recent dispute that you had with him about a mutual friend. In fact, Jack hasn't spoken to you since the dispute, which was several weeks ago. This thought brings up another association, the friend in question whose relationship with you has always been a bit rocky. That thought triggers emotions associated with that relationship. This thought then triggers thoughts and feelings about some other friends and your experience with friends in general. The sound of the horn from a red SUV has automatically triggered a cascade of thoughts and emotions, some conscious, many unconscious. But you can't leave it there; you have to make sense of the experience of the passing red SUV and the honking horn. You conclude that Jack was signaling to you a thaw in your relationship and so you decide to reach out to him later.

The fact that it wasn't Jack's car and the driver, whomever he or she may have been, was not honking the horn at you, is largely irrelevant.

Your mind had to create a story of the events and it did so drawing on associations and assumptions that were happening so fast – and were not available to conscious focus – that you could not verify them through rational System 2 thinking (as discussed below) or even some simple questioning.

The mind is an associative machine that is looking to make sense of the world rather than find the objective truth. The lens through which we see the world is our own experience tempered by the survival imperative and the fight-flight response. For example, in the story mentioned above, someone who is a little paranoid might not interpret the honking of the car horn as a sign of a thaw in the relationship but more as an aggressive gesture that signals the continuation of the argument. Our critical experiences shape the lens through which we perceive the world and they do this through the associations that those very experiences create.

What this means is that our narratives need to be consistent, because they are all based on our experiences, associations and each other. Using the same story above, if you have decided that Jack is an idiot and you never want to see him again, when you think he is honking his car horn at you, you'll assume that he is continuing to be a jackass. It would take an awful lot to convince you to have a positive view because that would mean literally 'changing your mind' and abandoning a previous narrative and discarding the 'gut feel' given to you by the fringe of consciousness. Which is exactly why changing one's mind doesn't happen as often as it should.

These dynamics have been researched extensively. Research in cognitive neuroscience has shown that our minds work in this intuitive way rather than being completely rational – or rational at all.

In his book *Thinking, Fast and Slow*, psychologist Daniel Kahneman shows how most thinking is intuitive rather than rational. He describes what I have outlined above as System 1 thinking – it is based on experiences, 'gut feel' and is often described as intuition. System 2 thinking is logical analysis, which is hard work and also requires at least a basic understanding of logic and statistics. Kahneman won the Nobel Prize in economics for showing that the prevailing model of a rational economic man who always made the best rational investing decisions was not totally logical, but subject to System 1 dynamics as well as inbuilt cognitive biases. It turns out that the mind is not a logical machine but more of a storytelling one. Just because we have the capability of being rational doesn't mean that is our default setting. Our default setting is based on our experiences as mentioned above, not rationality. And of course, depending on your initial assumptions, logic can prove anything. If Jack really is an unfeeling idiot then the rational conclusion is that he is honking at you to mock you rather than acknowledge you.

In his extensive review of the cognitive neuroscience research conducted by himself and others, Kahneman highlights numerous cognitive biases which significantly impact thinking, perception and decision-making. For example, there is the *availability* bias, which means that if you can easily recall an example of an event you will overvalue its significance. For example, if you can recall several examples of ethical misconduct by politicians, you will conclude, wrongly, that ethical issues are more common amongst this group. Ethical misconduct by politicians is much more likely to get into the news and thus get your attention than other less high profile people, leading you to overemphasise its frequency among this group of people. The media therefore have an influence on your thinking by covering some stories more intensively than others and by not covering some stories at all.

Another bias is the *risk avoidance* bias in which people are much more likely to significantly err on the side of caution and overestimate risks. The availability and risk avoidance bias join together when, for example, there is a plane disaster. With traumatic photos and news footage constantly in view, the availability bias is accelerated and enhances the risk-avoidance bias. Many people immediately after an air disaster will say that they deem flying too risky and that they'll never fly again, despite the fact that rationally, the odds of a plane crash have not been altered by one accident. Other biases are in play in this scenario, too. The 'recency' of the accident means that we overreact; in a month's time our views about flight safety probably have reset to where they were before the accident.

Other better known biases include the *Halo Effect*, in which one positive characteristic becomes over generalised to all perceptions of a person, and *Hindsight*, in which we rearrange our narratives to match the known outcome.

Another important bias is the mind's tendency to be binary – or think in terms of either/or alternatives. It's natural, when considering an issue, to think of two competing ideas when in reality there might be several and the ideas might not be mutually exclusive. This leads to several other difficulties, like assigning weight to specific ideas. For example, what's more important to health, eating right or exercising? That question is a false dichotomy and a misleading one. These two activities are not mutually exclusive and indeed, they influence each other; your nutrition needs will be based on the type and level of activity you engage in.

Our stories are, therefore, significantly influenced by inbuilt biases with, at most, a passing nod to reason. Kahneman's view is that when we interact with the world, we operate mostly on System 1 'intuition' and 'gut feel' and only do a very cursory rationality check to ensure that our reactions can be justified. A detailed and thorough System 2 logical analysis is deemed not necessary, especially given that it is difficult, stressful and energy consuming.

Perception

Our narratives and their associations are the basis of our perceptions. These perceptions are the lens through which we see the world. When you view events through a lens you are imposing a meaning on what you experience. In neuroscience, this is called *top-down processing.* Your expectations colour your experiences and impose meaning. Processing that does not impose meaning on experience is called *bottom-up processing.*

There are several research studies into these processes, which can lead to what is called *attentional blindness.* In one study, where subjects played a simulation game in which they had to land a plane on the runway, commercial pilots actually landed the plane on top of another one that was waiting on the runway! The pilots simply didn't see the other plane because this was not part of their experience – they had landed planes many times and never encountered this scenario and therefore weren't expecting it.

"Reality is an illusion, albeit a very persistent one."–

Albert Einstein

Our perception therefore is *our* reality not necessarily *the* reality or one shared by others. Of course, we believe passionately in our reality and often have difficulty accepting another version. In fact, some people can't even entertain another version of reality.

What are the implications of this perceptual process for healthcare? One of the big implications is that your perceptions determine the meaning you attribute to events including health-related events including pain, injuries and disease.

Consider two retirees in their sixties who have just received a cancer diagnosis. How do they each perceive their health situation? One person, Nick, sees the diagnosis as a death sentence. He has had a fear of getting cancer for a while and now that he has the diagnosis he is convinced that his condition is terminal. As a young boy, Nick remembers watching his grandfather die of cancer and the devastating impact it had on his mother and the family in general. That thought and many emotional associations are influencing his narrative and perception. When diagnosed, Nick said 'it was his worst nightmare come true'.

Phil, on the other hand, sees the diagnosis as a challenge to be overcome. He generally has a positive outlook on life and is fairly even-keeled emotionally. He takes things in his stride and deals with the present rather than projecting too far into the future.

When Nick was told that the average life expectancy for his stage of cancer was about ten years, he assumed that he surely wouldn't live that long and that at most he might have 8 years left to live. When Phil was told the same statistic, he appreciated that it was only a statistic and that ten years was the average, which meant half of the people lived longer than that, and some lived at least another twenty or more years.

As a result of his perceptions, Nick is likely to be more stressed and depressed. As we have already seen, Nick's stress and depression are likely to compromise his immune system, which will impact his recovery. Later I'll show how these emotions can effect almost every cell in the body, again impacting Nick's immune response and potential recovery. Moreover, because of his perception and depression, Nick is likely to become more withdrawn, which will impact his mood and his thoughts. The more withdrawn he becomes, the fewer activities Nick does, disconnecting him yet further from potential sources of joy and purpose.

How will Nick perceive the chemotherapy treatment? If he sees them as part of an inevitable death march, how is he likely to feel before, during and after chemotherapy treatments? He is going to dread not just the chemotherapy but everything about the 'treatment', because it has a negative, deathly association for him. This will keep him caught in a very negative cycle, which on its own will cause pain, not only through muscle tension, but also through the action of discomforting emotions on his body. Nick will interpret the increase in pain as a sign that his cancer is getting worse, reinforcing his narrative that he is going to die. Nick's beliefs, which are not based on System 2 logic but System 1 'intuition', are almost certainly going to contribute to his demise.

Phil, on the other hand, is determined to continue to lead his life as normally as possible, and continue with a productive and meaningful retirement. As a result of his involvement with meaningful activities he will feel joy rather than stress, which will increase his immune system response, helping his battle against cancer. He will see his treatments, while difficult, as beneficial and positive, increasing their therapeutic effect. Continuing to lead an active life will mean that he is engaged and focused on productive actions, leaving him not just less time to be distracted by pain but an emotional state that will not increase his pain.

Descartes and sixteenth century Renaissance doctors might have emphasised the observable and deemed to divide the mind from the body, but that distinction is a false one; a cognitive distortion brought about by the bias of binary thinking. The mind and body are not two separate entities that mutually exclude each other. That distinction is a function of a bias that makes it easier for us to consider concepts as separate, rather than inter-related ideas. When a concept is named, like 'body' it exists in our heads as an independent idea. By naming it we have given it an individual identity and it is, therefore, easier to consider it as a single, separate notion. But just because it is easier for the human mind to work in singularities, doesn't mean that those concepts *are* singularities. Nonetheless, it is very easy, and maybe the default setting, for us to think as individual ideas which then lead naturally to false dichotomies, like mind and body. The fact is that mind and body are not just interconnected but they are also reflected in each other. And emotions have a large part to play in the mind-body connection, as we shall see in the next chapter. I like to use the term 'mibod' for mind and body, reflecting the unity and oneness.

Chapter 5

Emotions and Instincts

Chapter Five

Emotions and Instincts

"Your intellect may be confused but your emotions will never lie to you."

– Roger Ebert

If you have been following along on our journey with what I have been saying about the latest research on thinking, you will have learned that the narratives we create are based much more on emotions and instincts rather than logic. It takes a lot of effort and some skill to logically analyse every thought and idea we have. Instead, according to psychologist Daniel Kahneman, we go by gut feel with a cursory nod in the direction of rationality. Those gut feelings are driven by a combination of instinctive drives, like hunger and sex and emotions.

Instinctual drives come from the primitive brain and are concerned with survival, both at an individual and a species level. We need to eat, drink, defend ourselves and procreate. That's about as basic as it gets and those drives aren't really negotiable. How we act out those drives is another issue, but the drivers themselves are an essential part of being human.

Emotions, too, are a critical part of being human. They influence our motivation, drive our passions and can derail our efforts. They have a chemical basis that spreads their influence throughout the brain and the body. Feelings are based on social perceptions.

- Anger is based on the perception that you are being treated unfairly.
- Frustration is based on the perception that you are being thwarted.
- Guilt is based on the perception that you have violated some moral code.
- Shame is based on the perception that others believe/know that you have violated some moral code
- Anxiety is based on the perception that there is a threatening event upcoming in the near future
- Depression is based on the perception of helplessness

All emotions are signals that provide important information about your status. In that sense there is really no such thing as a 'negative' emotion. Sure, there are *uncomfortable* emotions but even in their discomfort they convey something important about your state. Having a primarily low state of mind is responsible for a high proportion of the problems people experience in today's world.

Emotions can be conditioned. Because they have important functions, emotions can be easily associated with cues, like places, things and people. For example, whenever you go into a certain place, you might feel anxiety or joy based on past experiences and associations. This is true of instincts, too. Because they have important functions they too can become associated with certain cues. In fact, the mind is programmed to associate certain behaviours with instinctive behaviour.

Prepared Conditioning

Have you ever had a taste aversion? This occurs when you eat a novel food, or something you rarely eat, and you get sick shortly afterwards. If this happens, you will have a taste aversion to that food that can last years if not a lifetime. Even the thought of the food can make you nauseous. That is because the body is wired to make the association between food and sickness, for obvious reasons. There is an evolutionary advantage in that animals that avoid foods that make them sick are likely to live longer. This is called a *hyper-prepared association* and is incredibly powerful. There are some associations that confer a survival advantage and these seem to be hot wired into the brain.

As far as taste aversions are concerned, it doesn't matter if you later discover that it wasn't the food that made you sick; that knowledge will do nothing to alter the taste aversion. If the food is not a novel food and is one that you have had many times before, your previous conditioning, i.e. eating the food and not getting sick, will offset the hyper-prepared response. In short, you already have a history with that food and thus the aversion doesn't occur, or if it does it is much milder and short-lived.

In some animal studies, a novel food has been paired with electric shock, rather than vomiting. Animals who have been shocked immediately after eating a novel food do develop an aversion but it is nowhere near as powerful as when they get sick. Food and electric shock is not a *prepared* association and therefore is not as powerful or long-lasting. This was one of the reasons why giving addicts electric shocks – a form of treatment at the Shadel hospital in Seattle during the 1950s – didn't work as a therapy. Making addicts sick after drinking alcohol might have been more effective but then again, alcohol is not a novel stimulus for alcoholics, so it wouldn't be very effective. In fact, who hasn't thrown up after drinking at one point in their lives? Rarely does throwing up after drinking have any sort of deterrent effect.

The point of all this is that instincts and emotions can have very powerful associations and these reactions can be stimulated by all sorts of cues and perceptions. However, much of the time, the associations and experiences that are driving the reactions remain below the surface of consciousness. They manifest as a general sense of discomfort with very specific symptoms, like anxiety. They are hard to pin down or identify. They are part of the *fringe of consciousness*, described in the last chapter.

Occasionally, an event will be so traumatic that it is etched indelibly in memory and rather than being part of the hidden fringe of consciousness becomes front and centre in the mind. These memories are the basis of Post-Traumatic Stress Disorder; they demand attention rather than living in the shadows, creating considerable distress. It is important to acknowledge that many people also experience Post-Traumatic Growth, where the experience empowers the person to go on and do great things – the key difference is the meaning that the individual has associated with the event or trauma.

The implication of these dynamics is that we need to manage and understand our emotional life and experiences if we want to control their influence on our thinking, decisions and behaviour. Without such a grasp on our emotional lives, we risk being led too much by an intuition that is based on emotional overreaction. And, because of the survival imperative, we are likely to be influenced more by anxiety than joy, fear rather than happiness.

The impact of the above not so good conscious and unconscious feelings on health is significant.

- The emotions impact not just the brain but the whole body through connections with the nervous, immune and endocrine systems.

- Physiologically they impact the immune system's ability to deal with disease

- They lead to pain and discomfort especially conditions like migraine, headache, back pain, muscle aches, fibromyalgia and so on.

- They impact thoughts and decisions and negatively affect lifestyle behaviours, leading to worse symptoms and even new health problems.

Impact of Emotions (and Thoughts) on the Body.

In her classic book, *Molecules of Emotion*, legendary scientist Candace Pert describes an informational system within the body that connects thoughts, emotions, the immune and endocrine systems. Pert argues that this molecular information system based on peptides that travel around the body and have the ability to interact with cells, effectively is a powerful connection between mind and body. In essence, she describes the infrastructure that does indeed connect mind with body.

Pert's ideas are fairly widely accepted and have been augmented by research in the two decades since the publication of her book. The field of Neuro-Psycho-Immunology (NPI) has expanded to show that mental activity does indeed have physical attributes that influence our bodies.

The key to this information system are cell receptors, which float on the cell membrane. One nerve cell might have millions of receptors so there is massive capacity within the system. A receptor is a single molecule consisting of strings of amino acids, often described as being like beads on a necklace. The receptor changes shape, making itself available to receive peptides that float in the fluids surrounding the cell. A chemical key to the receptor lock is called a ligand, almost all of which are peptides. Insulin, neurotransmitters like dopamine, and steroids like testosterone are all peptides. This information structure allows the nervous, immune and endocrine system to communicate and affect each other.

Pert coined the phrase 'molecules of emotion' after finding that about 90% of the neuropeptide receptors are found in the emotion centres of the brain, sometimes called the limbic system. These critical emotion structures include the amygdala, which is pivotal in modulating fear and the fight-flight response, the hippocampus, which manages basic life functions but also interconnects with the endocrine system, and other areas of the limbic system.

Researchers have been able to trigger strong emotions by electrically stimulating areas of the limbic system and especially the amygdala. Pert and her colleagues discovered that there were a lot of neuropeptides where sensory information enters the nervous system. Think about the fringe of consciousness described earlier and how those vague emotions exert an influence on focused sensory input. Pert's peptide informational system is an infrastructure that might explain how that is possible.

Immune cells also have receptors for all the neuropeptides, meaning that emotional information can influence the immune response and vice-versa.

As Pert says, 'using neuropeptides as the cue, our body-mind retrieves or represses emotions and behaviours'.

Pert argues that the system she describes means that memories, and thus emotional information, are stored in the body. Pert, therefore, believes that memory processes are driven by emotions, which are peptides.

"Peptides are the sheet music containing the notes, phrases, and rhythms that allow the orchestra—your body—to play as an integrated entity."

– Candace Pert

Memory and performance are, as suggested earlier, influenced by mood.

As Pert again states: 'Emotional states or moods are produced by the various neuropeptide ligands, and what we experience as an emotion or a feeling is also a mechanism for activating a particular neuronal circuit— simultaneously throughout the brain and body—which generates a behaviour.'

Pert believed there is one kind of peptide for each emotion. Endorphins, for example, mediate feelings of wellbeing, joy and bonding.

"Repressed emotions are stored in the body— the unconscious mind—via the release of neuropeptide ligands, and that memories are held in their receptors."

– Candace Pert

Emotions, then, have the role of being the interface between the mind and the body and as Pert says, 'are at the nexus between matter and mind, going back and forth between the two and influencing both.'

Immune cells make and secrete neuropeptides, the same brain chemicals that modulate mood and emotion. Through this mechanism the immune system and brain can communicate and influence each other.

This means, according to Pert, that 'emotion-affecting peptides, then, actually appear to control routing and migration of monocytes, which are very pivotal to the overall health of the organism'.

For example, in cancer, neuropeptides, which influence and reflect emotions, communicate with the cancer cell affecting it in a number of ways. Blocking the access of certain peptides would therefore influence the cancer cell's behaviour. The battle for access to the cell through the receptor of different peptides and even viruses, determines cellular growth and behaviour.

This amazing information system represents the interface of mind and body and shows the critical influence of emotional state on physical health. Pert believed that these processes could be influenced consciously, especially by such practices as visualisation, meditation and positive thinking.

If Pert is right, then managing emotions becomes a very critical part of healthy and happy living in general and dealing with pain, injury, disease and illness in particular.

Holding Emotions in the Body

James Pennebaker is an American psychologist who has spent his career researching what happens when people don't access and express their emotions. His work can be summarised like this.

When emotions are held, rather than expressed or understood, they impact physical health. Repeatedly, Pennebaker's studies done at the Universities of Virginia, and Texas, and Southern Methodist University, show that when people hold their emotions in, they have more subsequent physical illness as measured by a number of variables. His work has focused on the relationship between trauma, disclosure and health. Pennebaker has shown the value of expressing emotions especially through writing. Not only does his work show that expressing emotions is healthy but making sense of traumatic or different situations is also important.

Getting difficult emotions out would change the body-mind as described by Pert, and potentially influence the entire body. This is part of the reason why the Wescombe Method is so effective in changing people's lives.

The Impact of Emotions on Pain

Given the above it is perhaps not surprising that many practitioners have emphasised the impact of emotional state on the experience of pain. Freud held the view that emotional state could exaggerate the pain caused by tissue damage, or fabricate the sensation of pain – a form of hysteria. Even though it ran counter to the scientific and medical traditions of the time, there were some Victorian practitioners who understood the relationship between emotion, pain and recovery. For example, a famous British doctor, William Ostler, suggested that the recovery from tuberculosis, a major health issue in his day, depended more 'on what the patient had on his mind than he had on his chest'.

More recently, New York practitioner, Dr. John Sarno took Freud's ideas one stage further. He claimed that most back pain, and common muscle and joint problems, like repetitive strains, were caused by unconscious emotional states. Sarno argues that under unconscious emotional distress, the brain has the ability to reduce blood flow to certain parts of the body, leading to common pains and discomfort. For Sarno, unlike's Freud's theory of hysteria, the pain is real but of emotional origin. Of course, initially when Sarno aired his ideas almost 25 years ago, there was an outcry from the medical status establishment. If Sarno were right, the conventional medical wisdom that back pain was caused by all sorts of structural spinal problems diagnosed by expensive imaging, would need to be revised. The argument continues today but it is much easier now to go on YouTube and find several reputable physicians repeating, and even extending, Sarno's views.

If difficult and traumatic emotions exacerbate pain and disease, then reducing emotional discomfort should have a positive impact on health. Also, following Pert's lead, positive emotions should enhance health and recovery.

Moreover, it is not just that emotions can affect the body, they can affect lifestyle behaviours that affect the body. Depression, for example, often leads to lack of exercise, poor nutrition, lack of sleep and social isolation, all of which are associated with poor health, slower recovery and increased mortality. Depression is characterised by very low energy, which is bad for health. Stress and anxiety can do the same thing, adding fatigue and exhaustion to the unhealthy lifestyle behaviours mentioned above.

For so many reasons, therefore, emotions need to be managed effectively to successfully move from pain & injury to your ultimate health & happiness.

How to Defuse Difficult Emotions

There are various ways to defuse emotions and get it out of your body. I provide practical tools to help you do this in your bonus 42-Day Kick Starters Guide but for now I will describe different ways of managing emotions.

Meditation

There are numerous forms of meditation but most involve two critical components. The first is the slowing down of mental processing by narrowing focus onto one form of sensory input. For example, you might just focus on all the sounds you can hear, or just your breathing. The second component is the emphasis on experiencing rather than judging. For example, if you are listening to all the sounds you can hear, you listen with a view to experience not judge or interpret or even remember.

The value of meditation is that it trains your mind not to quickly, even impulsively, accept anything that comes into your mind. Theoretically, meditation allows you to be more discerning of your conscious state, allowing for a detachment that allows for less emotional reaction.

Studies have suggested that meditation does indeed lead to better emotional control. In fact, there is some evidence that long-term meditators have smaller amygdalas, the part of the brain responsible for emotion especially fear. There is also some evidence that meditation can increase compassion. It should be said that many of the research studies in this area lack enough subjects or controls but meditation remains a key way of managing emotions.

Journaling

As mentioned above, Dr. James Pennebaker is a champion of venting emotions, especially by writing and journaling. Journaling is a great way of expressing thoughts and feelings on a regular basis, and in a fairly unstructured way. The value of journaling is that writing is thinking and in the process of thinking, people can begin to observe, understand and make sense of difficult or traumatic experiences. Getting the emotions out instead of holding them in, is important. It is crucial to always write down all of the good experiences too, it will train our brains to habitually see the positive.

Talking it Out

Expressing yourself through conversation is also an important strategy. It is important, however, that the person you are talking to is receptive, encourages appropriate venting and can help you make sense of your experience. All of those are reasons why a qualified health professional is your best choice when talking out emotions. Moreover, a qualified health professional is independent and has no position or axe to grind unlike many of your friends or even family members. Expressing uncomfortable emotions is tough enough without having to worry about other people's reactions.

Talking it out does not mean constant repetition of your story or experience. A study by Byrd-Craven, Geary, Rose, and Ponzi who displayed a habit and encouragement of 'problem talk', as well as dwelling on the negative affect, leads to a significant increase in cortisol (stress hormone) – which feeds depressive states and anxiety over time. So the key is to limit the repetition of problem talk, ideally as early as possible to avoid strengthening neural pathways that will potentially create a destructive habit. I don't know anyone who would want to go back to a cinema to watch a terrible movie over and over again. Imagine how you would feel!

Relaxation Activities

There are a variety of activities that help relax the body and by implication, relax the mind. These include such activities as deep breathing, yoga, and deep muscle relaxation, all of which not only reduce muscle tension but also can actually slow autonomic arousal, reducing emotion and emotional symptoms.

Lifestyle Behaviours

There are behaviours that can facilitate emotional processing by creating a sense of wellbeing and increasing energy, an important concept in health. The obvious behaviours here are physical activity, especially aerobic and resistance exercises, healthy nutrition, and good quality sleep. The latter is very important and often underestimated both in prevalence and importance. It is estimated that many people do not get either enough sleep or enough quality sleep, impacting their ability to cope and wearing down the body's resistance. These are discussed more in the next chapter in the context of habits.

Purpose and Meaning

In addition to doing activities that can defuse and minimise difficult emotions like stress and depression, we need activities that actually promote positive feelings rather than just avoiding or neutralising tough and uncomfortable emotions. This raises the whole question of finding joy through service, purpose and meaning. Ultimately, leading a life of purpose and meaning will lead to less stress and more joy, fewer difficult emotions and more positive ones, and that can not only be good but great for your health as well as your happiness levels.

All of these ideas are great but the key question is how do you incorporate them into your lifestyle. And that raises the topic of habits.

Chapter 6

Habits

Chapter 6

Habits

"Our daily decisions and habits have a huge impact upon both our levels of happiness and success."

– Shawn Achor

What's the difference between a magician and a psychologist?

A magician pulls rabbits out of a hat and a psychologist pulls habits out of a rat.

Psychologists have learned a lot about habits in the last century and more recently this knowledge has been added to by brain research. Habits are important because they define our daily routines and therefore the degree to which we expose ourselves to all sorts of environmental elements, from sunshine to food to toxins. It is common to think of habits only as specific behaviours but don't forget that our thoughts can be habitual, too. And we have already seen how thoughts can influence our emotions and our bodies.

Every time you think, feel, or do something in a certain way you are stimulating and using a neural pathway. Our habits are the well-travelled pathways – established ways of thinking, feeling, and doing.

Imagine you have just moved to a country town and you want to get from your house to the local shop, which involves walking through a thick forest with no pathways. The more frequently you go through the forest the same way, the easier and quicker it will become to travel this pathway. It is the exact same way we create habits, both good and bad. Now imagine you had a holiday for a few months and then returned home. You decide to go to the local shop through the forest and discover it is harder and takes you more time. When an old neural pathway or a pattern of neural firing gets used less and less, it weakens. This is the process of rewiring, and is neuroplasticity in action. Repeated and directed attention towards your new way of thinking, feeling, and doing will create new pathways. Limiting or stopping the use of some of your current habits will cause those pathways to weaken and become less powerful.

The importance of habit cannot be underestimated. Not only does habit train the brain and body to act in certain ways, habit provides the repetitive exposure that creates many of the health problems that are common today. For example, a small amount of sugar is not inherently bad but when you have small amounts of sugar five times a day, every day for years, the cumulative effect can be devastating. And habit is the process by which you build cumulative effects, be they healthy or fatal.

As we have already seen, the brain is a very trainable organ. If you do the same action over and over, the connections and pathways that underpin that action get more and more established with repetition. To change that action you have to work very hard to undo those brain pathways and connections and establish new ones. A child still has many potential brain connections and pathways but even by adolescence, some of the potential connections and pathways are 'pruned' making newer connections more difficult to create. That process continues so that by the time you are into the mid-thirties it becomes even more difficult to create new connections. Changing is more difficult than it was as a child but of course, still very possible.

There is a difference, however, between learning something new, like the London taxi drivers who were memorising the streets of London and showed brain changes as a result of their learning, and *unlearning* a behaviour. For example, it is common experience that changing a well-entrenched behaviour like smoking, or eating sugar, is extremely difficult. A well-entrenched behaviour like smoking becomes well established, so that it is associated with a variety of social, environmental and internal cues. Exposure to those cues, stimulates the urge to smoke through association and memory. These associations also have a physical basis in brain pathways. Exposed to a cue that is associated with smoking – for example, having a cup of coffee – the brain will immediately register that this is a smoking situation and the body anticipates incoming nicotine and the other substances in a cigarette. As a result you have the strong subjective experience of wanting to smoke as your brain and body conspire to create the temptation.

The difficulty of changing a habit that involves the ingestion of a substance like tobacco or sugar is compounded because of the withdrawal symptoms that occur when you have a temptation and do not fulfill it. With the continued use of a substance like tobacco, the cells in your body develop a tolerance to the tobacco, which results in two important outcomes. First, as a result of cellular tolerance, your body needs more and more of the substance to get the same effect. This results in escalating use and increased tolerance, creating a vicious cycle of use. The second result of increased cellular tolerance is withdrawal. If you do not indulge when you have high tolerance, the cells go into withdrawal, increasing the desire to indulge even more. This is also sometimes called *functional tolerance.*

These typically are measures of what is called physical dependence. It is important to note that physical dependence is not an all-or-nothing concept. Rather, physical dependence is seen as a continuum, so one can be mildly, moderately or severely physically dependent. While it is tempting to assume that this tolerance and withdrawal dynamic only applies when substances like tobacco are involved, there is some evidence that feelings of withdrawal and difficulty stopping also occur when no substances are ingested. For example, compulsive gamblers report withdrawal symptoms of discomfort, anxiety and even physical symptoms like nausea, when they try to inhibit their gambling behaviour. While gambling doesn't involve the ingestion of substances, presumably brain chemistry is altered by the addiction that creates both psychological and physical feelings of 'withdrawal' when the behaviour is inhibited.

The concept of psychological dependence, which is also seen as a continuum, refers to the degree to which non-physical cues can stimulate a desire for a substance. Severe physical and psychological dependence tend to go together, but it is possible to be severely psychologically dependent and less physically so. It is important to understand how environmental factors can be on these processes. In a study conducted almost forty years ago, rats who were withdrawn from a narcotic in the cages where the narcotic was consumed displayed severe withdrawal. Other narcotic-dependent rats who were withdrawn in novel cages not associated with narcotic use, showed significantly fewer withdrawal symptoms. Most people who have tried to quit smoking will attest to the fact that it is often easier to quit when they are in novel situations that have no association with smoking.

Long-term behaviours, therefore, are extremely difficult to change. There was a famous study in the 1970s that showed the success rate was similarly low, regardless of what behaviour was the focus of change. The success, or more accurately, the failure, rate for behaviour change was similar for those trying to quit drugs, lose weight, and quit smoking. Subsequently, there has been more research that shows the probability of long-term, maintained change of entrenched behaviours like those mentioned above is very low, between 10% and 20%. Recent research suggests that the failure rate might be even lower. One recent report of thousands of people trying to lose weight by changing lifestyle behaviours suggested that long-term success rate was nearer 1% than 10%. The key here is the notion of *long-term maintained changes* not fleeting or temporary ones.

Research evidence and experience suggests that people can make short-term changes to important lifestyle behaviours like nutrition and exercise, but typically these are not maintained. They are not maintained for several reasons.

First, it is possible to change your environment and behaviour in the short term. But the plethora of strong cues associated with the habit can't be avoided forever and sooner rather than later you are overwhelmed by a cue that stimulates physical and psychological desire to indulge in the habit. For example, it is common experience for people who attend a rehab clinic to have a much-reduced desire to indulge after they have gone through withdrawal and remain in the safe confines of the inpatient unit. However, once they return home, the cues can be overwhelming and lead to much greater temptation and, as a result, relapse.

Second, the brain is lazy and unless it is in a threatening situation, prefers to conserve rather than use energy. Under those circumstances after a few days you start thinking of great reasons why you need to resort to your old behaviour.

Third, the brain lives in the present and discounts the future. So if your weight loss goal is to look great for that family reunion in four months time and you encounter some of your favourite chocolate cake right now, the cake is going to win.

Fourth, motivation is driven by emotion not logic. Having good reasons to lose weight or quit smoking is all very well and good but unless you have a very strong emotional connection to those reasons, you don't have much of a chance of changing your behaviour. For example, someone might decide that they need to lose weight because they have been told their excess weight is bad for their health. Another person wants to lose weight because they have just had a heart attack in which they almost died, and have been told losing weight will make another coronary less likely. Who is more motivated and more likely to succeed in their weight loss?

All of this raises the question of how long does it take to change a habit. You might have heard that it takes 21 days to change a habit. Oh, if it were that easy!

Obviously there are differences in habit strength. Some people might have smoked two cigarettes a day, while another might smoke 40 a day. Interestingly, the number of cigarettes smoked is not necessarily a reliable measure of dependence. For example, people who smoke 40 cigarettes a day usually only take one or two puffs per cigarette, while a much 'lighter' smoker might smoke each of their ten daily cigarettes right down to the butt. I have a friend who works in a quit smoking clinic and he told me of a case when a heavy smoker celebrated having cut back from 40 cigarettes to ten a day. However, when his levels of carboxyhemoglobin, a stable complex of carbon monoxide and hemoglobin that forms in red blood cells upon contact with carbon monoxide, were tested, they were no different. He was smoking the ten cigarettes four times more intensely than the 40!

People vary in their levels of physical and psychological dependence. Someone might be mildly physically dependent but still very psychologically dependent. People also vary in their motivational levels and degrees of social and environmental support. So numerous variables impact the odds of any one person successfully changing a habit. One of the reasons why the Wescombe Method has had such high success rates for changing people's lives is the trained health professionals ability to help each client create a strong emotional connection between them and their motivations for change. This step is extremely powerful when combined with the professional support, accountability and coaching by the health professional.

If you do the same behaviour every day for 21 days you will have established that behaviour in your repertoire. However, the question really is how *robust* is that new behaviour? Will it endure if you stop doing it for a day or two, or a week or two?

The fact is that you have to do a new behaviour for a long time to get to the point where it is robust. Let's suppose you start to exercise. After 21 days of exercising you have the beginnings of a new habit. But if you stop for a week, the chances aren't that good that you'll pick it up again. In fact, you probably have to do a new behaviour consistently for at least a year to establish it as a habit that won't disappear if you stop it for a few days. So the 21-day concept is a myth, I'm afraid – if you are trying to replace an old well-entrenched behaviour. On the other hand, if you are simply trying to establish a new behaviour, rather than replace an old one, then 21 days may be long enough to get it started in a meaningful way.

So habits are critical influences on our behaviour that go a long way to shape our bodies, brains, moods and overall health. Establishing healthy behaviours is therefore a critical part of avoiding disease and also living your best life possible. Most diseases today are not lethal viruses. The big threats to our health are created by poor lifestyle behaviour and habits that are very difficult to break once established. Diabetes, coronary heart disease and dementia are all significantly influenced by the behaviours we do every day.

There are four key lifestyle behaviours that will have a major effect on your health and happiness. If you establish the right habits in these areas, you will be taking care of yourself. You have the choice and the control.

Here are the four main areas that influence health and where having the wrong habits can doom you, not just to poor health but your happiness, too.

Exercise

Human beings were designed to move – and not by car. There may be animals that are faster but human beings have endurance and stamina that allow them to go longer and further. This has been a huge evolutionary advantage, allowing homo sapiens to survive and thrive. If we don't move, however, our bodies and our brains suffer.

There is, of course, tons of evidence of the advantages of exercise. Exercise burns calories. Aerobic exercise strengthens the cardiovascular system. Exercise is the best stress obliterator. Exercise encourages the growth and maintenance of new brain cells. Resistance exercises develop muscle, build endurance and are associated with the increased production of BDNF – brain derived neurotrophic factors, which are important for healthy brain function.

Establishing and maintaining a healthy exercise program is probably the single biggest thing you can do for your health and happiness. This means:

- Establishing an aerobic activity habit, be that jogging, walking, swimming, cycling, or combinations of these.

- Establishing a resistance exercise routine using weights – ideally with a qualified health professional to help you achieve the correct movement patterns for your body type and also to enjoy the accountability for cementing new habits

- Establishing a mindset of activity, for example, not sitting for hours at a time, leisurely walking or movement in addition to the activities above and finding opportunities to use your body, e.g., take the stairs rather than the elevator.

As we have seen earlier in the chapter, the sooner this is established as a habit the better. Parents have a responsibility to develop this habit in their children. You can start an exercise program in your 60s and it does confer some advantages but the fact is that it will be so much easier, the younger you can get into the exercise habit.

Nutrition

Eating habits represent the biggest source of prolonged exposure to potential toxins. Most people in the world eat three times a day every day. If you are eating healthy foods, this will represent constant exposure to beneficial compounds that can influence every aspect of your body and brain. Foods provide the basic building blocks of our body, so poor nutrition is the equivalent of slowly poisoning yourself. Saturated fats and sugars are the worst culprits, especially the sugars that are hidden in so many foods. Sugar consumption has a direct impact on type 2 diabetes, which is a precursor for cardiovascular disease, stroke and dementia.

Many people think that good nutrition is about limiting calories. It isn't. Good nutrition begins with eating healthily, which means fresh not processed foods, fruits, vegetables, and modest amounts of dairy, meats and fish, and a minimum intake of sugar.

Establishing healthy food choices is tough especially if you have been used to eating unhealthy foods for a long period of time. The answer is to go slowly to ensure that changes are established before you try to institute new ones. I know people who get frustrated with their diet and decide they are going to change it all tomorrow. No sugar, no desserts, no alcohol, 1200 calories a day, only fruits and vegetables and so on. It is about impossible to change all of those things at once so you are doomed to fail. There is more on the specifics of how to change your diet in the bonus 42-Day Kick Starters Guide.

Sleep

Poor quality sleep is an underestimated problem. In the busy lives that people lead, it is easy to sacrifice sleep for the constant processing of the wired world. Millions of people of all ages do not get quality sleep on a regular basis, which is seriously problematic. Lack of sleep leads to low energy, which is a major health issue. Lack of energy can sabotage your best efforts at managing other important lifestyle behaviours. For example, poor quality sleep has been linked to obesity. Think about it, if you are tired you look to food to boost your energy. If you're tired your level of self-control will be much less than if you are full of energy, probably leading to poor food choices like sugar. Fatigue reduces the energy in the brain, leading to fuzzy thinking and decision-making and low mood states, like frustration and irritability. Frankly, it's difficult to be happy on three hours sleep. And how do you think a lack of energy will influence your most important relationships in life?

The amount of sleep people need varies a little from person to person but the range within which most people fall is six to ten hours, with eight being the average. Young children need a little more. Sleep is critical in that it recharges the brain and body, as well as organising and processing memories and the experiences you have had during the day.

In the bonus 42-Day Kick Starters Guide there are tips and tools for ensuring you get quality sleep. These tools include the timing and types of food eaten later in the day, ways of relaxing in order to get into sleep mode and ways of turning on the sleep cycle.

Stress Obliteration

As you have already learned, stress can be a killer in its own right. It can hijack the immune system, rendering the body's defense system vulnerable to attack from all sorts of pathogens. High levels of stress, poor exercise, sleep and nutrition, can make lifestyle changes all but impossible, trapping you in a downward spiral and cycle of ill health. You certainly can't be happy when you are under chronic stress. The brain and the body's resources are used to hunker down and survive the threat, often leaving you exhausted. When in a chronic stress, it's like you are either running on full or running on empty with nothing in between. You go from fired up to exhausted very quickly, as the brain works at max levels before crashing. This is one reason why anxiety and depression very often go together.

Of course, it is unreasonable to expect a stress-free life. I live in Scarborough, Western Australia – it is a popular beachside suburb and a common place for surfers to gather due to the regular waves. Each wave coming in can be seen as a life challenge – we know there will always be more coming, it is guaranteed, but we have complete freedom of choice of how we prepare and respond to each one. A wave might knock us down, but we can choose to stay down or get back up again. We may even choose to surf a wave and enjoy it, or dive straight through and obliterate a few.

Acute stress is going to occur for everyone – challenges are a normal part of life. But when managed properly or obliterated, acute stress is not a health issue. There are numerous ways of obliterating stress. There are a range of relaxation techniques that reduce physiological and brain arousal, and it is important that you master at least one of these. These include such techniques as meditation, yoga, deep breathing and other similar activities that involve shifting your focus and changing your physiology. As you will see in the 42-Day Kick Starters Guide, eliminating negative thoughts as well as surrounding yourself with supportive people, is also critical. And the three other behaviours mentioned above, exercise, nutrition and sleep, all have a role to play in effective stress obliteration.

All of these four key behaviours affect each other, your mood and your ability to be happy. A good exercise program is a huge stress obliterator and gives you the energy needed to fuel positive thoughts and emotions. The same can be said of nutrition and sleep; proper levels enhance, energy and wellbeing. And all of these elements lead to better obliteration of stress.

These core behaviours then are the underpinnings of health and wellbeing, but what about happiness? Do these behaviours ensure happiness in themselves, or is something else needed? That is the subject of the next chapter.

Chapter 7

Happiness

Chapter 7

Happiness

"Happiness cannot be traveled to, owned, earned, worn or consumed. Happiness is the spiritual experience of living every minute with love, grace, and gratitude."

– Denis Waitley

In the previous sections we have looked at the contribution of emotions, thoughts and habits to health and concluded that emotional control, positive thinking and healthy habits all contribute to wellbeing. But where does happiness fit into the picture? Does health bring happiness and does happiness bring health?

What is happiness? That is an age-old question with many, varied answers. We use the word 'happy' in many different ways. For example, we ask people whether they are 'happy' with a particular outcome or circumstance. In that sense the word 'happy' really means pleased – that we are satisfied with an outcome. Happy is also used to describe a temporary state. If we're having a good time at a social event, for example, we might look or feel 'happy'. But most people who have thought about the subject at all say that happiness is not a temporary feeling. We might feel good when we are having fun but that is not happiness. That is a feeling of pleasure, and pleasure is distinguishable from happiness.

"The uppermost level of happiness is experienced when we appreciate our past mistakes and successes, combined with positive anticipation for the future."

– Scott Wescombe

In her survey of Happiness around the world, Carol Graham describes 'miserable millionaires' and 'happy peasants'. Her survey addresses a key issue in the understanding of happiness: the role, or lack thereof, of material wealth.

It is easy to see why many people equate happiness with money. Money would appear to alleviate many common stresses. Financial stress is all pervasive and influences every aspect of one's life – something that I know first-hand. For many people, finances constitute the major stress in their lives and they therefore assume that the absence of such stress would mean that they would be much happier.

"Happiness is when what you think, what you say, and what you do are in harmony."

– Mahatma Gandhi

With more money, people are indeed likely to be somewhat less stressed. However, less stress is not the same as happiness. It might be difficult to be happy under continued stress, especially financial stress, but the reverse is not the case, i.e., less stress does not equal happiness. Many wealthy people are miserable. Admittedly, their money often allows them to suffer in comfort, but again money does not equal happiness. In fact, there are many wealthy people who are depressed and lost, and they will categorically tell you that you cannot buy happiness. So it's a logical fallacy to assume that happiness is about money.

Remarkably though, many studies have proven that the way you spend money, and as little as five dollars a day, can make you happy. Tony Robbins highlighted a study by Harvard's Elizabeth Dunn and Michael Norton in his book *Money: Master The Game.* Robbins writes that 'every day spending choices unleash a cascade of biological and emotional effects that are detectable right down to saliva', and 'while having more money can provide all kinds of wonderful things – from tastier food to safer neighborhoods – its real power comes not in the amount but how we spend it'. According to Dunn and Norton's research, the top three ways of spending for massive boosts in your happiness levels are investing in experiences, buying time for yourself, and – a mammoth one – investing in others. It has been proven the more you give to others, the happier and healthier you are.

"'Material strivings' (i.e. goals for fame, fortune and success) have been repeatedly shown to detract from well-being and are more likely to lead to psychological and personal problems."

– Suzy Green

If happiness is not really about money, what is it about? In Carol Graham's research, the happy peasants were people who often had very little in terms of material wealth. Instead, they had stability in their lives, roles that were meaningful and enjoyable, and were often surrounded by strong, loving and stable relationships. Moreover, many of these people had simple lives with not much opportunity for change. And that brings up an interesting point about modern society and change.

R.D. Laing has argued that the more complex society has become the more stressed and neurotic people are. As people have more and more choices, they have more and more expectations. If you live in a very structured society with very defined roles, the argument goes, then you don't spend your time chasing dreams and life becomes a lot simpler. And amongst some groups that stability translates into happiness.

Many people would argue, however, that structured situation is not happiness but limitation and it prevents people from striving to better themselves. Ignorance is not the same as happiness.

What Carol Graham has picked up is not that striving for self-improvement is a bad thing but that one has to separate striving from purpose and the chase from meaning. What appears to have happened is that in Westernised first world culture, material striving has become the main, and sometimes only, goal for some people. And when that happens other important aspects of life, like purpose and meaning, get devalued, or even worse, ignored.

People are social animals and are constantly comparing themselves to others. This comparison tendency means that many people are trying to keep pace or ahead of their neighbors in material possessions and wealth. That becomes their main goal in life ahead of any other more enduring and substantial values. When that happens there can be no real happiness. There is always someone else, richer than you to envy and to compete with.

Money is just a token. It would be nice if it represented value, but it doesn't. There are all sorts of ways people can acquire money: hard work, brilliance, inheritance, crime. Striving for money is not the same as striving for value.

The flipside of the human beings social nature is that we are all connected, or have the potential to be. We are wired to feel empathy and compassion. We have specific circuits in the brain – mirror neurons – that allow us to identify what others are thinking and feeling. There is debate about the purpose of this ability. Some philosophers argue that this ability to connect with others is a purely rational decision by human beings who understand that cooperation is sometimes necessary for survival. Other species, so the argument goes, are not capable of such reasoning and therefore don't show the same levels of empathy and cooperation.

"If you want others to be happy, practice compassion. If you want to be happy, practice compassion."

– Dalai Lama

However, other experts dispute that connectedness is the sole prerogative of human beings. In his excellent book *Primates and Philosophers*, primatologist Frans de Waal shows that other primates also show empathy and what is called 'theory of mind', the ability to interpret what others are thinking and feeling. De Waal cites an experiment that could not be conducted today but was permissible over 50 years ago. In this study there were two apes in separate cages. When ape A was fed, ape B received a painful electric shock that made him cry out. Under these circumstances the apes who were getting the food actually refused to eat, often to the point of starvation. In one case an ape refused food for twelve days.

De Waal also cites other examples of animals displaying theory of mind. In another example, a famous zookeeper found that the only way she could get a baboon off the roof, where it frequently went, was not with food or other enticements. The only way the zookeeper could get the baboon to come down was when she pretended to be crying and in distress. Then the baboon came instantly. De Waal provides other examples of primates consoling each other and generally showing compassion.

Most people who have pets lower down the evolutionary scale than primates, will attest to the fact that their animals seem to be attuned to their owner's human emotions. It would seem that compassion is not just a rational construction of human beings but deeply ingrained in the animal kingdom. Presumably, animals that stick with each other, help each other and develop community are more likely to survive than a bunch of individuals. In fact, helping others and by so doing elevating the community, is probably one of the most universal and hard-wired behaviours. There are exceptions, of course, but for most people doing something that benefits others is a highly rewarding behaviour. And it is rewarding not just externally, by the appreciation of others, but also internally with positive feelings.

When people are bonding, in other words engaged in positive social interaction that bear all the hallmarks of the interactions described above – helpful, compassionate, etc. – there are various chemical reactions that occur in the body.

Oxytocin has been described as the 'love hormone'. It is the chemical responsible for the feeling of pleasure that one gets when engaged in a very positive social interaction, or what in the broadest sense might be called a 'loving action'. Oxytocin not only has calming properties and makes one feel at peace but it also has other potentially healing properties. For example, oxytocin has anti-inflammatory properties. Inflammation is implicated in many major illnesses and diseases including cancer, dementia and heart disease. Any anti-inflammatory agent therefore has a huge bearing on health and wellness.

Dopamine is a neurotransmitter, which has several functions, mostly to do with motivation and pleasure. Dopamine is typically released whenever there is any pleasurable behaviour. So dopamine is involved in pleasure associated with all sorts of behaviour, from eating to sex, from drug-taking behaviour to risk taking. Dopamine then seems to be associated with temporary feelings of pleasure rather than happiness. However, other neurotransmitters do seem to be more associated with happiness than pleasure. One of these is the neurotransmitter gamma-aminobutyric acid or GABA. GABA is the neurotransmitter most associated with a sense of peace, rather than pleasure.

The evidence therefore points to the fact that social connection in general and taking actions that benefit others in particular, is not just psychologically satisfying, it is physically healthy. Through neurochemicals such compassionate action lead to positive changes in the brain and the body. As I mentioned in the chapter on emotions, Candace Pert argues that our emotions influence the massive communication that goes on throughout the body. Negative emotions can translate into negative energy at the cellular level, positive emotions can manifest in positive cellular energy with consequent benefits that resonate throughout the nervous, endocrine and immune systems.

Compassion, empathy and compassionate action, therefore, are psychologically and physically good for us.

When you consider real values, almost all of them revolve around the idea of doing good, not just or even for yourself, but for the enhancement of others. Enhancing the community in some way, providing service, helping others, are examples of important values. Greed can be a guiding principle but most people wouldn't consider that a *value*. One of the most common conflicts in modern society occurs at the interface of profit and service. For a company, striking the right balance between profit and service is critical. If a company is seen to be only concerned with profit, even at the expense of service, then it is likely to be viewed with cynicism and scorn. The most successful corporations are those who make their profits by providing service to their customers rather than exploiting them.

It is very easy to lose sight of the bigger picture of our behaviour. We go about our daily duties, focused on the specifics of our actions and without focus on what those actions really mean. There is the famous story of three men working on a religious building site. A man approaches each of the men and asks them what they are doing.

The first man is laying some bricks for a wall.

'I am laying bricks,' he says when asked about his actions.

The second man is mixing cement.

'I am mixing the cement for this wall,' he says, when asked about his actions.

The third man is carrying bricks across the site to where the other two men are building a wall. He is asked what he is doing.

'I am building a cathedral,' he says with pride.

It is so easy to forget when we are building cathedrals. The work can be slow and painstaking and we are likely to focus on the small picture right in front of us rather than the bigger picture right above us. You'll note that the third man derives his meaning by being connected to a much greater value and purpose. In business circles today that might be called being more engaged – owning the value and meaning of the task.

"Remember that the happiest people are not those getting more, but giving more."

– H. Jackson Brown

This distinction in perception between the micro aspects of the task and the macro meaning of it is a key to success and happiness. If you are just doing a job for the money, if you are experiencing the actions of the task as something that has to be done before the end of the day, if you are focused on the minor details, you will not see the big picture. If your perception is of doing a job rather than serving a purpose, the job will seem boring and perfunctory. If you see your life like that, too, as a series of things that have to be done in order to pay bills, buy that car, a series of obligations to meet financial ends, it too will lack real purpose. There will be what I call *the meaning disconnect.* When you suffer from *meaning disconnect* life will be boring, joyless if occasionally punctuated with moments of pleasure.

Well, you might say, I don't have much meaning in my life. I have a boring job and not enough money. But you might also be a friend, a parent, a sibling, a neighbor, a colleague, and a member of the community, all of which are extraordinarily meaningful roles.

"Happiness is nothing more than good health and a bad memory."

– Albert Schweitzer

This speaks to the subject of what Mihaly Csikszentmihalyi (Six-Cent-mihaly) calls 'Flow'. Flow is a mental state where one is doing an action almost without thinking and experiencing the meaning of it rather than merely watching yourself doing it. Flow helps you stay connected to purpose.

When you are focussed on the meaning of your activities and they are purposeful then you will automatically be in a state of gratitude. An attitude of gratitude is a positive mindset. A positive mindset generates positive energy, which flows throughout the body and into every cell, in the manner described earlier.

If happiness is about being connected to activities that have meaning and have a bigger purpose, how do you ensure that you build that into your life?

Part of the answer is to stay connected to the meaning of the activities that you do and to see the big picture rather than get obsessed with the details. Another part of the answer is to spend at least some time in activities that are plainly done to help others or the community at large. These include volunteering, charitable gifts and other service activities.

"The happiness of most people is not ruined by great catastrophes or fatal errors but by the repetition of slowly destructive little things."

– Ernest Dimnet

Happiness is not the same as temporary pleasure. Happiness is about meaning and purpose and it has a profound effect on psychological and physical wellbeing.

The simple universal equation I created for a persons happiness levels after interacting with and helping thousands of people all over the world from different countries, cultures, religions, and backgrounds, is:

Your Level of Gratitude

+

Your Level of Positive Anticipation

=

Your Happiness Level

The great news I have for you is both gratitude and positive anticipation can be enhanced through our daily practices. Barbara Fredrickson states there is a happiness set point given at birth, which accounts for about 40% of our happiness. Research findings display positive events (i.e. winning the lottery) and negative events (i.e. a spinal injury) change our happiness levels in the short term, but eventually we return back to the baseline (happiness set point).

For a long lasting boost in your daily happiness levels or your happiness set point – you must include practicing gratitude and positive anticipation as a part of your daily rituals. As we discussed earlier, through neuroplasticity and creating habits, happiness levels can be elevated. The more you and I practice, the more connections the neurons in our brain form, and that area of the brain grows and gets stronger, like building a muscle.

At the start of this chapter I asked questions about happiness and health. The best answer I can give you was in a meta-analysis study titled 'The Benefits of Frequent Positive Affect: Does Happiness Lead to Success?' which included over 200 scientific happiness studies and 275,000 people worldwide. They found happiness leads to success in all areas of life. These areas included health, work, marriage, friendships, sociability, energy, and creativity. The worlds leading happiness experts, such as Shawn Achor and Alexander Kjerulf, also support these findings. So happiness is essential to your ultimate health!

In the next section you and I will consider how social interaction facilitates happiness – and health.

Chapter 8

Love

Chapter 8

Love

"When top scientists and psychologists talk about what's important to our overall wellbeing and how satisfied we are with our lives, the only thing that they all agree on is that social relationships are probably the single best predictor of our overall happiness."

– Tom Rath

In the last chapter I looked at the value of gratitude and finding meaning and purpose as a basis of happiness and health. In this chapter I will consider the contribution of positive personal interaction to happiness and health.

Love in its broadest sense comes in many forms. It can come as friendship, support, family relationships and romantic love. The *Oxford Dictionary* definition of love is:

> 'fondness, warm affection; sexual passion; sweetheart or loved object; enamored; pay amorous attention; engage in sexual intercourse; be in love with; feel affection for; delight in; admire; like to see.'

While many of those pertain to romantic love, the last four are about love in its broadest sense. Love is a verb not a feeling, entailing actions that represent mutual nurturing. Love, in its broadest sense, has been shown to enhance health. There are many examples in the medical literature.

The Healing Power of Love

For example, David Spiegel researched the role of support in response to cancer treatment. He specifically looked at the role of support for those with breast cancer. He and his team investigated women all undergoing the same treatment for breast cancer. There was just one difference between two groups undergoing the same medical treatment. One group met in a support group once a week for a year where the focus was the experience of having breast cancer. The women shared their fears, hopes and experiences.

The results surprised his research team. When Spiegel looked at the data after five years he expected that the support group would impact the breast cancer patients' *quality of life* but have no impact on their longevity. Instead, he found something quite different. The women who had been in the support groups lived twice as long as those who hadn't.

One of the participants in Spiegel's study described the role of support like this:

'It is very different to worry about dying at 3am in the morning by yourself than it is to talk about it at 3 in the afternoon with nine other women who have the same problem you do. It makes the stress different. I have no doubt at all that it helps people live better and I think the evidence is accumulating that it helps them live longer as well.'

Spiegel had this to say about the role of support in dealing with disease.

'The power of group support makes tremendous sense to me. We're social creatures and the brain enables us to form connections with others and build networks of support that help us stay alive, that help us deal with threat, that help us nurture our young, and create stable and relatively safe cultures. And that social connection, especially in the face of illness, I think is a very powerful ally. It helps us manage our stress responses, help our bodies do better, and help one another get through life-threatening situations.'

Support groups are probably the biggest behaviour change agent. When they work properly, they provide accountability, which is essential for any life change. Support groups also provide the opportunity for members to share advice and information as well as to connect emotionally and allow for venting of emotions, which is an extremely important health behaviour. Support groups also provide others the chance to remind you of your motivation and reasons for change when you have lost sight of it.

"A friend is someone who knows the song in your heart and can sing it back to you when you have forgotten the words."

– Albert Camus

Unfortunately, very few support groups and support group leaders are given training in how to effectively run a group and so a lot of the time, the group runs by default. Nonetheless, when run properly, a support group can be an incredibly valuable part of anyone's journey of change. This is an important component of the Wescombe Method – having trained health professionals to serve as the leaders to facilitate optimal outcomes.

"Unconditional love is the most powerful health asset a human can possess."

–Scott Wescombe

The Power of Social Interaction

Social interaction is powerful and has a much greater influence on us than we imagine. The impact of interaction manifests in a number of ways.

Mirror neurons were first identified about 20 years ago by Italian researchers working with macaque monkeys. They found that when the researchers performed an action, the areas of the brain that are used in doing that same action, were also stimulated in the macaque observing the behaviour. A similar system of neural circuits was later identified in humans. These circuits seem to be responsible for our innate ability to identify with another person. In social interaction we are constantly consciously and unconsciously assessing the mental state of other people. What are they feeling? What is their motivation? As mentioned earlier, this is called 'theory of mind' – we are trying to understand another's mental state. Sometimes, through the mirror neuron circuits, we actually feel what we think they are feeling. We are thus capable of empathy and compassion.

What we see others doing, therefore, has a direct impact on our brains. More recent research suggests that this theory of mind mechanism extends not just to reacting neurologically to what we see people doing but even to what *we hear* them saying. In these studies, brain reactions were observed in subjects who were just listening to another person describe an action. So, for example, if someone was not falling over but just *talking* about falling over, listeners' brains reacted as if they were experiencing falling over. So, we respond automatically not just to the sight of an action but just hearing about an action.

The impact of these mechanisms that are driven by identified circuits in the brain is that our emotions, and then our thoughts and even behaviour, are heavily influenced by what we see other people doing. Our social interaction significantly determines our mood.

If you question the impact of others on our moods and emotions, consider these scenarios.

You sit down to talk with an acquaintance. Unfortunately, he is having a hard time and wastes no time telling you about his troubles and woes. He describes how stressed he is. He goes into detail about the latest disasters in his life. As he is talking, you can see that he is getting more and more upset. After ten minutes of this conversation how do you think you will be feeling? Chances are pretty good that you will be feeling a little stressed, maybe even a little depressed and possibly frustrated.

Now let's suppose you sit down with another acquaintance. Life seems to be going well and he is very upbeat. He is smiling and laughing and telling you about all the fun stuff he has been doing recently. He describes his successes and adventures with energy and verve. After ten minutes of this conversation how do you think you will be feeling? Chances are pretty good that you will be feeling energised, upbeat and in a positive mood.

Hopefully, you can see the tremendous power of social interaction. It can elevate our mood and along with that positive affect comes a change in biochemistry and physiology for the better. Is it any real surprise that David Speigel found that the support group affected longevity as well as life quality?

Social Proof

In addition to powerful effects on mood and emotion, what we see others doing also influences our behaviour. This is called 'social proof' – we look to others for not just validation of our behaviour but for what we should be doing. Have you ever seen someone looking up at the sky? What's your reaction? You're likely to look up in the sky, too, even though you might have no idea what it is that you are expecting to see! You're driving down the freeway and everyone passes you going a whole lot faster than you are. What are you likely to do? There's a good chance that you will speed up, too.

Social proof has been used to explain the apparent aloof and cynical behaviour of people when it comes to helping another person. If you were walking down the street and saw someone lying on the sidewalk, what would you do? If you were alone you might very well stop and try to help or at least determine whether any help was necessary. If other people had stopped and were helping there's a chance that you might stop and ask if they needed your assistance. But what would happen in this situation if there were a lot of people walking by the prostrate person and nobody was stopping to do anything? If everyone were just ignoring the body on the sidewalk, what would you do? The chances are that you, too, would walk on by. In this situation, you would probably rationalise your actions with some thought like, 'they must be okay, otherwise other people would be stopping to help'.

Social proof is a huge driver of our behaviour and we are often unaware that it has even been so influential.

Have you seen Derek Sivers' Tedx video 'How to start a movement?' It is available on Youtube (www.youtube.com/watch?v=V74AxCqOTvg) and shows what happens at a music festival when one person gets up to dance. The first person gets up and starts dancing and we might think of him as the leader. But nothing happens for a while until two other people join in. They are critical. Before long others get up to dance and in a matter of minutes everyone is up dancing!

The leader may have been the first guy to dance but no doubt he could easily be dismissed as a loner or a weirdo. But when others get up to dance they validate the action and make it acceptable to join in the dancing. Now an onlooker is not just joining one person, he or she is joining in many people. In fact, it reaches a tipping point where if you are not up and dancing, you're in the minority!

The short video is a great example of social proof in action. Within a few minutes, everyone has got up to dance because one person started and then others joined in. Hundreds of people change their behaviour. Now they are all happily dancing and moving their bodies.

We have the power to influence others. We have the power to lift people's spirits, to inspire and motivate them, too. Not only do other people's actions influence our emotions they change our thoughts and behaviour, too.

"Happiness is determined by factors like your health, your family relationships and friendships, and above all by feeling that you are in control of how you spend your time."

– Daniel Kahneman

So through interaction with others, our mental states, thoughts, emotions and behaviour can all be influenced. And given the power of social interaction, especially positive social interaction, it's no surprise that it features as one of the cornerstones of health. In general, the research literature suggests that the more sociable a person is, the healthier they are likely to be. Whether it's measured by the quality of personal relationships, or the number of relationships, the findings strongly suggest that good social relationships are associated with good health. These findings apply to general health and even specific health issues like dementia. Recent studies suggest that an active social life is a key to preserving brain health, delaying and possibly postponing the onset of Alzheimer's Disease and other dementias.

Dean Ornish is a well-known American cardiologist who espouses healthy lifestyle for prevention of heart disease. Despite all of his encouragement and work about adopting healthy lifestyles, especially nutrition, Ornish says that the single biggest factor in preventing heart disease is – love. Ornish defines love in its broadest sense as a reflection of positive meaningful relationships. Like David Spiegel, he, too, finds that positive relationships and health go hand in hand.

Relationships and Happiness

Our relationships aren't just a source of health they are, of course, a source of happiness, too. Relationships might just be the most meaningful aspects of our lives. In her book, *The Five Regrets of the Dying*, Bonnie Ware identifies that one of the biggest regrets that people have on their deathbeds is that they didn't invest more time in their relationships. As they look back on their lives, people identify their relationships as one of the most important aspects of life. Indeed they are. This was backed up by a 75-year longitudinal Harvard University study, called 'The Grant Study', which found relationships had the greatest positive impact on life satisfaction. George Vaillant who was in charge of the study for a few decades stated, 'Happiness is Love. Full Stop'. Where would you be without your relationships?

"We need to have intimate, enduring bonds; we need to be able to confide; we need to feel that we belong; we need to be able to get support, and just as important for happiness, to give support. We need many kinds of relationships; for one thing, we need friends."

– Gretchen Rubin

Relationships are a two-way street. It's not just what you get from another person it is also what you give to another person that provides meaning and purpose. As I mentioned earlier, giving in its various forms is the basis of happiness and given the power of personal connection, you can hopefully now see why.

"We invest less in our friendships and expect more of friends than any other relationship. We spend days working out where to book for a romantic dinner, weeks wondering how to celebrate a partner or parent's birthday, and seconds forgetting a friend's important anniversary."

– Mariella Frostrup

Like many other aspects of life, many of us manage our relationships by default. We let them drift, don't put in the effort, allow them to slip away without any attempt to save or even resurrect them. It is critical to invest in them otherwise you might end up like one of Bonnie Ware's subjects – at the end of the day regretting not putting more into arguably your most valuable asset.

Romantic Love

Up to now, I have been talking about love in its broadest terms. What about romantic love? That wonderful infatuation phase of a romantic relationship typically marks our happier if not happiest times. As the relationship grows, by necessity, it has to move out of the infatuation phase into something more permanent and meaningful – a loving friendship that is built on mutual respect, caring and nurturance. It is no surprise that people in a romantic relationship are healthier than single people.

"The single most important factor in our long-term happiness is the relationships we have with our family and close friends."

– Clayton Christensen

Happiness and health both depend on the number and quality of your social relationships. In the bonus 42-Day Kick Starters Guide I give some suggestions on how to ensure you have a rich and full social life and an abundance of social relationships.

"Health is the greatest gift, contentment the greatest wealth, faithfulness the best relationship."

– Buddha

Chapter 9

How to #behappydaily

Chapter 9

How to #behappydaily

Happiness is a choice. It doesn't just come to you, like a surprise gift from the sky. It is something you create every moment of every day. If you can't be happy in *this* moment then you probably can't be happy in any moment. And once you create happiness in this moment, you will every day develop the happiness habit. And make no mistake happiness is a habit.

"Be happy for this moment. This moment is your life."

– Omar Khayyam

The happiness habit requires you to take action every day so that the critical parts of your life are aligned and functioning to optimise your wellbeing. In many ways, just like love, happiness is a verb that is about doing rather than feeling. And when you do the right things, happiness will be yours.

You can't be happy if you are constantly fatigued and lacking in energy. You might want to be happy but you will be overwhelmed by exhaustion. Energy is an important part of happiness just as happiness is an important part of energy.

You can't be happy if your body is not functioning up to its amazing potential. This includes your brain, too. So the lifestyle behaviours that provide energy and optimise health and wellbeing are critical to happiness. These include proper nutrition, exercise, sleep and the best stress obliteration tools.

Happiness also entails feeling good about yourself. It is tough to be happy if you can't look yourself in the mirror and know that you are managing every aspect of your life the best way you can. You can't always achieve your expectations or be successful in the way that you hoped. Self-esteem comes not necessarily or even from success. It comes from knowing deep down you are giving everything in your life your best shot and not avoiding decisions and actions that are difficult or uncomfortable. The path to happiness often goes through uncomfortable.

As well as taking care of your health, happiness is about taking care of your mind. Happiness comes from an active decision to view the world positively and not get caught up in stress and negativity. Happiness comes from a determination to manage your focus, attention and reactions.

The decision, mindfulness and commitment to be happy by adopting these behaviours are needed every day. Just like any other habit, the longer you practice happiness, the more likely that those happiness habits will become a part of you. But a habit only develops with constant daily exposure and repetition. The happiness behaviours, the lifestyle habits of nutrition, exercise, sleep and stress obliteration and the determination to maintain a positive focus, foster relationships and see the meaning and purpose of your life, all require a daily focus.

In the earlier chapters I talked about learning and how the adaptable brain can be modified, sometimes dramatically, with constant exposure. When you practice happiness every day you are changing your brain. You are creating new connections and pathways in your brain with repetition and practice. You seriously can change many aspects of yourself, including perspectives and thoughts, with constant repetition.

"Positivity alters the brain and changes the way people interact with the world."

– Barbara Fredrickson

I have already mentioned the four key lifestyle behaviours of exercise, nutrition, sleep and stress obliteration. I will review them again here with specific reference to their role in developing happiness.

Exercise & Posture

Exercise will serve many functions that are important for happiness. Aerobic activity will give you the energy you need to maintain focus as well as being an integral part of stress obliteration. It will enhance a positive mood both physiologically and psychologically. By balancing neurochemistry and actually producing endorphins, aerobic activity can produce a positive physical effect. Not only will that help you psychologically, but the fact that you are working out and taking care of your body will improve your self-esteem. There's the self-esteem measure again: can you look yourself in the mirror and honestly say you are doing everything you can to take care of yourself? If you are not exercising and taking care of your body, there'll always be part of you that knows you are not doing everything you can.

Resistance exercises can help preserve muscle, strength and even balance. A good resistance regimen will also boost confidence as well as muscle mass. More specific suggestions on exercise routines are provided in the bonus 42-Day Kick Starters Guide.

Our posture, which refers to the positioning of our body, can literally make us confident or depressed. Can you describe to me the difference in postures between a happy and unhappy person? I am sure you can! The way you position yourself creates changes in your body that can change the way you feel. A popular study by Amy Cuddy revealed the impact posture has on our biochemistry – with certain postures decreasing cortisol and increasing testosterone, setting people up for greater success in life. You can watch Amy's Ted Talk on her findings here: https://www.youtube.com/watch?v=Ks-_Mh1QhMc

The typical daily postures we adopt, both static and dynamic, also determine how our bodies will function today and in the future. Static posture refers to how we position ourselves when stationary – sitting, standing, kneeling, sleeping etc. Dynamic posture refers to how our bodies move when we go from sitting to standing, walking, running, jumping etc. Factors that can influence posture include muscle strength and conditioning, movement patterns, the environment, nutrition, water intake, sleep pattern, and state-of-mind.

Pain and injuries caused by the affects of accumulative poor posture account for a high percentage of the people I have treated, fixed, and enhanced over the past decade. Consistent poor posture each day, whether it is static and/or dynamic, can cause repetitive micro-trauma to structures (muscles, tendons, ligaments, bone, nerves) of our body. At some point, the pain sensitive structure may reach a threshold, whether it takes 20 minutes or two years, and start sending pain signals back to the brain saying, 'I have had enough, I am in pain, stop irritating me and I will stop irritating you'. This is what we call acute pain – but when the structures continue getting irritated the pain or injury can become chronic, which means it will usually take longer to eliminate. If it's taken two years to develop versus 20 minutes to hit the threshold – it will take much more time and effort to fix. Think about a pathway in the forest, the difference of walking the same track for two years versus 20 minutes – which one will grow over quicker? So even if you are not in pain now, I strongly encourage you to optimise your posture to help reverse the potentially destructive changes and maximise your life performance.

One of the biggest driving forces of poor posture is the increase in sedentary behaviour. It includes sitting or lying down doing activities such as playing computer games, watching TV, driving a car, and reading. Over recent decades in Australia and other first world countries, there has been a transition from jobs requiring a high-energy output to a low-energy output. Jobs have gone from construction, farming, and manufacturing to the majority now sitting at a desk. From an evolutionary perspective we were designed to move and engage in physical activity continuously throughout each day. Our postural muscles simply decondition when they are not stimulated regularly, which can lead to stress on pain sensitive structures – the same can occur when people adopt rigid, stressed or abnormal postures. The same muscles that help protect and keep our spine healthy, allow us to walk and run better, safely lift and carry objects, and can also help prevent overload on structures along the kinetic chain.

Being sedentary has been labelled as the new smoking due to the real consequence of an earlier death from cancer, heart problems and other chronic conditions. Even if you exercise for 30 minutes per day, but sit for the rest of the day, you are exposed to the same risk factors. There was a London study published many years ago that found bus conductors, who spent the majority of their typical work day walking up and down the bus as well as up and down stairs, experienced half the amount of heart-related mortality than the bus drivers who spent their day sitting behind the wheel. The key message is to move your physical body more often; it will make you happier and help you live longer!

Our physical body is made up of trillions of cells and it is the vehicle that allows us to experience life. Each cell represents a soldier in your happiness army of life. They communicate with each other constantly, respond to your environment and to the signals they receive from what you do. Different groups of soldiers make up parts of your army like your tissues and organs. If your soldiers aren't operating efficiently you can experience a breakdown in the functioning of your physical body. Understanding how to nourish your army with exercise and nutrition is the first step to creating the energy, postures and physical body you desire to flourish in this life.

Each soldier plays a variety of roles in your army everyday, including keeping your DNA safe from damage and providing energy for everything you do. Your DNA is stored within the nucleus of your soldier. A poor diet low in antioxidants and phytonutrients (your weapons and ammunition) – and high in environmental exposure to toxins (the enemy) can cause your DNA to become damaged. When damage occurs to your DNA, it affects the ability of your soldiers to produce energy and can cause them to die early resulting in inflammation or compromised tissue. There has also been some links that this damage can show up as cancer years later. The good news is if you consistently nourish your army, they will keep you healthy, happy and looking younger for many more years.

Just like there is a recipe for baking an amazingly healthy chocolate cake, there is a best-proven recipe for nourishing and providing your army with optimal firepower for happiness. Every day thousands of new soldiers are replicated from old ones. New soldiers replace old soldiers that become worn out or damaged. It is your job to provide your army with the raw materials for the creation of new soldiers.

Nutrients from your food make up the raw materials and are one key aspect of how what you eat plays a role in sustaining your soldiers happiness, and therefore your army. Energy is produced for your army via your mitochondria (thousands inside each soldier). The mitochondria utilise the nutrients from your food and oxygen to create energy. Exercise increases the number of mitochondria you have per cell, thus enhancing your ability to produce energy. It's important for you to note - what you consume can either kill your soldiers or make them happier and stronger – it is your choice.

Nutrition

Nutrition will influence the state of your mind and body and is, therefore, a huge contributor to your happiness. There are many diets and nutrition plans and schemes that promise to help you lose weight, feel good and achieve health. Even accepting the fact that we are individuals with slightly different needs, patterns are emerging from research, which suggest healthier ways to eat that apply to everybody.

The biggest problem with a typical western diet is not just the amount of food, it's the fact that the food is processed. Processed food contains chemicals, preservatives and other toxins, which are unhealthy for several reasons.

First, some of the ingredients in processed foods are simply unhealthy for you. These include trans fats and hydrogenated oils that have been linked to vascular disease, which includes not just heart disease but also dementia. In addition, many processed foods contain sugar, which some experts argue is more damaging to health than fat. As I have already mentioned, the consumption of sugar has skyrocketed in the last century and is directly related to obesity, diabetes and, some experts now argue, to dementia.

In addition, processed foods are by definition processed in the factory not by your body. As a result, the ingredients are typically rapidly absorbed leading to spikes in blood glucose levels, which stimulate hunger and more eating in the long term. This is the problem with the so-called high glycemic 'white foods' like pasta, bread, and confectionery. They spike blood-glucose levels, often rapidly, which has a detrimental effect on energy and mood, as well as stimulating more eating. It's tough to be happy when you are feeling lethargic after that meal loaded with high glycemic carbs – i.e. processed carbs, or 'white foods' that are rapidly absorbed.

As a result of these problems, the almost universal recommendation for improving diet is to avoid processed foods and eat fresh foods. I know a famous gastroenterologist who says that the best advice he gives to clients, some of whom are candidates for weight loss surgery, is to cook at home. When you cook at home, not only do you have control over what you're eating, the food is likely to be much fresher than eating out.

Another important aspect of cooking at home concerns the oil used to cook foods. Olive oil is considered the healthier choice but many restaurants still use partially hydrogenated oils, a trans fat, because they can be used repeatedly and are thus cheaper. So that food might look healthy on the menu but if it has been made with high fat cooking oil, it's not so healthy, after all.

In any event, eating fruit, vegetables and other fresh foods and avoiding processed, fried foods as well as severely restricting sugar is the best nutrition plan. Fresh fruits and vegetables are the basis of any healthy diet. They contain fibre and as a result are passed efficiently through the intestines. One thing to be mindful of is the sugar content of fruits and vegetables compared to processed foods. The sugar in fruits and vegetables is typically slowly absorbed compared to processed foods. It is also different, typically sucrose rather than fructose. Moreover, even though the sugar content of some fruits is high, it is important to look at how much of that is *bio-available* or *bio-accessible,* in other words actually absorbed by the body. You might look at the sugar content of a fruit and think that it is high but remember some of it simply is not bio-available and passes right through the system.

A diet high in fresh fruits and vegetables and very moderate in dairy, meats and even fish is not only healthy for you it will give you the energy needed to maintain your happiness focus. Interestingly, recent research suggests that The Mediterranean Diet as well as vegan diets seem to protect against vascular disease and dementia. We will be hearing more about this in the coming months and years, I am sure.

What you put into your body on a daily basis will eventually impact your health, your energy and your happiness. There are some more nutritional recommendations in your bonus 42-Day Kick Starters Guide.

Sleep

As I identified in the earlier chapter on this subject, good quality sleep is another factor in health, energy and wellbeing. Millions of people go about their business each day seriously sleep-deprived. Sleep deprivation not only leads to poor mental functioning but low energy that makes it difficult to make the happiness choices and implement the behaviours that are necessary for happiness. For example, as I have mentioned, insomnia is associated with obesity. When we are fatigued it is more difficult to make healthy food choices and instead we are more likely to reach for the processed foods, which give us a quick fix of energy but actually lead to more and worse calorie consumption. In addition, poor sleep takes away the energy you need to make good decisions, not just about food, but other important lifestyle behaviours and decisions in your life.

In general, our thinking reflects our physical and emotional state. Let me repeat that – *our thinking reflects our physical and emotional state.* When you're angry you think angry thoughts. When you're fatigued, your brain and mind just want to conserve energy and rest and thus make life as easy as possible. When you're happy, you think happy thoughts.

Poor sleep patterns and sleep apnea, in which airways become blocked during sleep leading to frequent waking throughout the night, are both associated with increased cardiovascular disease and dementia.

Quality sleep is essential for us if we are going to have the level of control over our thoughts, emotions and behaviour that are critical to happiness. It is difficult to lead a life of purpose and meaning if you can't stay awake. I have included specific recommendations for getting the quality sleep you need in the bonus 42-Day Kick Starters Guide.

Stress Obliteration

Some of the behaviours above contribute significantly to effective stress obliteration. A good exercise regimen, healthy nutrition and quality sleep all provide the energy required to obliterate stress. However, there are also some other very specific behaviours that can give you control of thoughts and emotions, allowing you to take a balanced perspective and developing a sense of peace even when life is not going the way you had anticipated.

I have already mentioned meditation and other 'alpha state' activities, like yoga and deep breathing, that enable you to calm your mind and not get caught up in stressful processing and worry. These are critical and it's important that you develop at least one of these skills and practice them on a daily basis. These relaxation procedures also allow you to do something else that is essential for happiness: analyse and manage your thinking.

Manage Your Thinking

One of the most important messages that I give my clients is that our thought process is influenced by our physical and emotional state and is based on our personal experiences. As a result we have a very individual perception of the world that can be based on temporary states and old thinking habits that may be wrong, or irrelevant. Earlier in the chapter on Thoughts, I mentioned psychologist and Nobel Prize winner Daniel Kahneman's *Thinking, Fast and Slow* which wonderfully summarises cognitive research and concludes that our thoughts are more individual and 'intuitive' rather than logical. In order to find happiness we need to not just understand our thinking process but learn to manage it.

It is difficult, some might say it is impossible, to be objective about one's own thinking. So many of our narratives are based on false perceptions, simplistic assumptions and overgeneralisations that form the core of our beliefs about the world and our selves. It is important for us to look at these narratives and ideas and analyse them more carefully. Thoughts and narratives can be extremely self-limiting as well as wrong.

"I am determined to be cheerful and happy in whatever situation I may find myself. For I have learned that the greater part of our misery or unhappiness is determined not by our circumstance but by our disposition."

– Martha Washington

For example, a young adult male acquaintance of mine is always striving to achieve. He works hard in his job as an engineer, he works out fanatically, and seems to hardly have any time to relax and enjoy life. He has never experienced 'flow' and the joy of the moment, but rather is always in 'processing mode', analysing his performance, anticipating all the other actions he has taken in the day, and never feels he has made the grade. He is a perfectionist who is striving so hard to get everything right that he has no time to be happy. His thought process, decisions and behaviour are based on the notion that he has to be perfect to be happy.

You can never reach happiness like that. For one thing, his brain is so wrapped up in the stress of doing, that he loses out on the joy of experiencing. And incidentally, when your brain is in this constant processing, Beta wave state, it is not very capable of being innovative and creative, which is associated with a more relaxed, unfocused alpha brain wave state. His brain is quite literally always in overload, which never gives him a chance to unwind to a much more, relaxed and peaceful state, or to step back and be innovative. He has never learned how to relax.

When he reaches his limits, he crashes. He is either going full speed or he is stopped. Until he changes that fundamental perception about himself, he is doomed to remain in that cycle and never experience peace. He needs to re-evaluate his thought process and the stories he tells himself. He needs to investigate where those ideas came from and how they limit his life. He also needs to learn to live in the present, to actually experience 'flow' and the different mental states of relaxation and peace.

Many of us are similarly trapped in the cycle of doing, racing from one activity to another, not really experiencing or enjoying anything. Happiness is not completing a to-do list.

Examining self-limiting beliefs is very important if you want to find happiness. Indeed, some people have the belief that they will never be happy and then set out, consciously or otherwise, to sabotage anything that might put them on a path to a happier future.

Another way in which we trap ourselves is by dwelling too much on the past. When we get stuck on past hurts or failures, we lose the moment we are in. Living in the past inevitably means failing to appreciate the present. We can't allow the past to ruin the moment.

"The first recipe for happiness is: avoid too lengthy meditation on the past."

– Andre Maurois

Is Happiness a Choice?

It is often said that people 'choose to be happy'. What that phrase means for me is that people have conscious control over their thinking and make the deliberate decision to focus on the positive and purposeful and not allow self-limiting and negative beliefs to take root. And it is much easier to do that when you have the physical and mental energy derived by following the lifestyle behaviours described earlier.

Getting control of your mind and having the ability to see and then eliminate negative and self-limiting beliefs often requires the help of others, more specifically health professionals who are objective and are trained to help us see the errors in our thinking and, more importantly, how to change them.

Controlling your mind is not just about eliminating negative, self-limiting beliefs, it is also about having a positive mindset, and there is a difference. For example, the perfectionist client mentioned above might ease up on his perfectionism and learn to slow down but that in it self would not necessarily make him more positive. It would certainly be a step in the right direction and make a more positive mindset more likely but in itself slowing down is not the same as developing a positive outlook.

What is at the core of a positive outlook? In my view, there are two critical components.

The first is to have the conscious control so that you do not overreact to events. Remember the cognitive biases mentioned in the chapter on thoughts? When emotionally laden events happen there is a danger we are going to overreact to them. The fact is that we don't know what those events might mean. Our brains will overreact and imagine worse case scenarios, and if we're not careful we find ourselves embracing them automatically. The key in this situation is not to bury your head in the sand but to recognise that the meaning of the event has yet to unfold. Sure, you might have fears about what might be happening, but they are fears not realities. I am reminded of a great quote by the Danish philosopher, Soren Kierkegaard:

"Life can only be understood backwards but you have to live it forwards."

In other words, we don't really know the meaning of events when they happen. There certainly have been times in my life when I have thought, 'Oh no, this is the worst thing that could have happened', and it turned out to be a genuine blessing. Conversely, I have had times when I thought something was a huge blessing and it turned out to be a bit of a curse – but still served a purpose and contributed to the person I am today. Of course, how events turn out are also a function of how we approach them. If we think that something is going to be a disaster, it probably makes disaster more likely.

"Success is not built on success. It's built on failure. It's built on frustration. Sometimes its built on catastrophe."

– Sumner Redstone

The other important perception is to believe that things are possible. Rather than developing self-limiting beliefs we need to foster self-affirming beliefs. We need to see obstacles as challenges to be overcome rather than barriers that stop us. We develop resilience and a 'growth mindset' not a fixed one. We need to see failure as a critical learning experience on the way to success.

So understanding and managing your thought process is a key to happiness. In the bonus 42-Day Kick Starter Guide, I provide more practical details of how to develop a healthier, happiness mindset.

Everyone has the opportunity to be happy. It requires effort, focus and commitment on a daily basis but the pay-off is enormous.

"Far better is it to dare mighty things, to win glorious triumphs, even though checkered by failure... than to rank with those poor spirits who neither enjoy nor suffer much, because they live in a gray twilight that knows not victory nor defeat."

– Theodore Roosevelt

Chapter 10

#TheNewRich

Chapter 10

#TheNewRich

"If you laugh, you think, and you cry, that's a full day. That's a heck of a day. You do that seven days a week, you're going to have something special."

– Jim Valvano

The quote is from Jim Valvano who was a very successful and colourful American college basketball coach. Valvano was struck down in his prime by cancer. In 1993, he gave a very moving and often shown speech at a major sports awards, in which he advocated living life to the fullest and appreciating every moment (you can see it here at www.youtube.com/watch?v=HuoVM9nm42E.) Shortly afterwards, Valvano died but his legacy lives on. His cancer research fund has raised more than $130 million and his legacy continues.

When Valvano is talking about living life to the fullest, he is talking about being authentic. He is talking about feeling the experience of every moment, whatever that moment is. He is talking about living with honesty and openness. After all, that is real freedom. Happiness is the ability to be open to experience life to the fullest extent.

"It is not how much we have, but how much we enjoy, that makes happiness."

– Charles Spurgeon

The connection between wealth and happiness has already been discussed. The reality is that money does afford you some opportunities, especially time, which can be used to develop the sort of happiness mindset that I have outlined throughout this book. But money on its own does not buy happiness. For many people, money simply allows comfort but not happiness. On the other hand, financial stress is all-pervasive, its tentacles reaching into every area of life. And there's no question that financial stress can make life difficult. So for sure, money makes life easier. But easy isn't the same as happy.

Happy is about being fully engaged in life. Happy is about being able to live in the moment, to enjoy the 'flow', to experience the richness of life as outlined by Jimmy Valvano. When you are able to experience life at that level you will almost certainly feel grateful. You will also feel connected to the world, rather than living in the unhealthy cocoon of your own ego. You will be outer directed and service-oriented. And when you are outer directed and service oriented you will find purpose, meaning and even a legacy.

"If you've got a billion dollars and you're ungrateful, you're a poor man. If you have very little but you're truly grateful for what you have, you're truly rich."

– Sir John Templeton

I have known many extremely wealthy people who have no sense of direction. Without the need to find a job they drift along comfortable - but direction-less. Overall money and happiness are two separate variables that are often unrelated.

You don't need money to develop the happiness mindset. What you and I have found is that happy people can come from any culture and any walk of life, as Carol Graham identified in her report on Happy Peasants and Miserable Millionaires. We discovered that happiness is associated with health and wellbeing. What we will find out on our journey is that as Bonnie Ware identifies in the *Five Regrets of the Dying,* at the end, life is not about money or possessions, it's about relationships, service, and meaning.

"Happiness is not something ready made. It comes from your own actions."

– Dalai Lama

Money is the common currency and I suppose it's natural if also misguided to view money and material possessions as the way in which we measure ourselves. But surely the immaterial is more important; how we feel every moment, how we feel about ourselves, how we nurture and develop relationships with our fellow human beings, how we contribute.

If I told you that I could grant you one of two wishes. You could either be happy every day or have ten million dollars, which would you choose? Of course, those options are not mutually exclusive alternatives but for the purposes of comparison, which would you choose?

Hopefully you agree that those who are happy are the richest people.

"Be happy with what you have and are, be generous with both, and you won't have to hunt for happiness."

–William Gladstone

Barbara Fredrickson supports this concept with an impressive amount of research, and has summarised the benefits of experiencing happiness and other positive emotions for your physical body. These include a better immune system, less pain, less stress, lower blood pressure, better sleep patterns, fewer colds, lower risk of diabetes and stroke, faster production of new cells in your brain and body and a longer life. This is what I call being 'rich'. I invite you to invest your time, money, and efforts to boost your happiness 'currency' – the greatest and most valuable asset in your life – take action today!

"To be rich, is to #behappydaily"

– Scott Wescombe

Final Words

Wow, what an amazing journey we have taken together, wouldn't you agree? I have a deep respect for you and your commitment to raising the standard of living for yourself and the people around you. It's been a privilege and honour for me to be able to serve you and facilitate your growth throughout this nourishing journey together.

For me, this journey started over a decade ago at 18 years of age, when I became a qualified personal trainer – my aim was to help people create healthy changes in their lives for the better, following my own transformation in my late teenage years. With high standards, passion, perseverance, and dedication – an exercise and sports science degree, physiotherapy degree with first class honours and dozens of other qualifications later, as well as learning from some of the best people on this planet, combined with real world experience of transforming thousands of people – I have been able to create this wholehearted gift for you. My wish is you will create the health and happiness you deserve and desire, so that you too can pass this gift onto others.

If you want to awaken all of humanity, then awaken all of yourself.

If you want to eliminate the suffering in the world, then eliminate all that is dark and negative in yourself.

Truly, the greatest gift you have to give is that of your own self-transformation.

– Lao Tzu

By joining the Best Body movement you will be largely celebrating the unknown impact you have on peoples lives. My greatest celebrations in life to date have been for having the courage and companionship to achieve results in the future for clients. Preventing individuals, families, and communities from unnecessary suffering by moving them in a different direction today. At the same time, enhancing the life performance for more happiness, joy, love, and inner peace. Our greatest contribution will be what did not happen to the people we love and care about the most – for me that is every single person on this planet, including you. Grandparents will be there for weddings, to help gardens flourish without weeds, to babysit and tell stories to their grandchildren. Parents will not miss out on seeing their kids graduate, getting married, having children, enjoying birthdays and Christmas celebrations. Children will not miss out on the unconditional love, support, and guidance from their parents and grandparents – they will not have to witness the people they love suffering or living a poor quality of life in advance or unnecessarily – they will not learn it is normal to helplessly struggle through life.

You may have had experiences like me to already be able to see, feel, hear, and know the impact of missed opportunities in people's lives, people that you admire and care about. If not, I want you to bring the future forward, focus on two different pathways, a sub-optimal and optimal one. Close your eyes – focus, feel, hear and see the difference between the two pathways. Notice the difference in your life and all of the people you care about. Think about how you will spend those extra quality years, who will you see, where will you visit, and what will it feel like? How many more places will you get to experience? How many more lives will you positively impact? Who will be smiling? Choose to maximise your health and happiness – you will be leaving a valuable legacy behind for future generations.

I believe the healthiest, happiest, and most grateful people in our world are the most valuable people on this planet for taking consistent daily action that, either directly or indirectly, positively influences every single person around them. I am guessing you are one of these people by reading this book. According to Shawn Achor in his incredible book *The Happiness Advantage*, we do create a ripple effect that infects everyone around us within three degrees – which is about 1000 people for the average person. Imagine that – you get healthier and happier – and at the same time you are positively impacting approximately 1000 people – pretty awesome, right?

The ripple effect can occur in a negative fashion as well as positive. This is one good reason why it is crucial you become aware of who influences you – are they nourishing or slowly poisoning you? The common saying is you are the average of the three to six people you spend the most time with. Some experts call this the process of digesting sensory food – what we hear, see, feel, and consume – and it can have long lasting effects.

"We make a living by what we get. We make a life by what we give."

– Winston Churchill

I have talked about the changes that you need to make for your ultimate health and happiness throughout this book. In this section, I am going to give you the steps to start to make it happen. The Wescombe Method will work for you – it is proven. To get started you just need to follow the steps below.

At every stage of life you are in a dynamic state of change – what you think, feel, and do each day will either make you healthier and happier or unhealthier and depressed – notice what is happening now, are you trending upwards or downwards? The finest thoughts, actions, and daily behaviours – and being consistent – do not change regardless of age. At certain stages of life there are some considerations, but the essentials remain the same.

At the start of our journey together I shared the formula for you to reach your ultimate health and happiness goals –KNOWLEDGE + ACTION + SUPPORT. Some of the information you will receive in the 42-Day Kick Starters Guide that you may have already downloaded will not be new to you, but regardless of people being aware of it – from my experience only about 12% of us eat enough vegetables and about 17% of us move enough.

"To LEARN and not to do is really not to learn. To KNOW and not to do is really not to know"

– Stephen Covey

This is a very important concept because it is easy to allow ourselves to get sidetracked. In almost all of the reputable research the groups who perform best in terms of health are the ones who adhere best to the guidelines. For example, sugar consumption is extraordinarily high in first world countries, responsible for many of the chronic diseases, like diabetes. Fizzy drinks are extremely high in sugar, some of them containing the equivalent of 16 teaspoons!

Let's suppose you are used to drinking ten fizzy drinks a day, thus ingesting an incredible 160 teaspoons of sugar just from these drinks. Now, suppose you decide to cut back and reduce your fizzy drink consumption by half – to five a day. You might feel proud of your effort and self-control. However, you are still consuming a very unhealthy amount of sugar through these drinks. So, as noble as your effort has been, it might have made very little difference to your health and disease risk. So cutting back fizzy drinks from ten a day to five is great IF you are then going to cut back from five to two, ideally on your way to giving them up altogether, or drinking them very infrequently. This was the process I went through as a teenager, going from drinking multiple litres of Coke per day and no water, to no Coke and litres of water. Let me tell you my life was never the same again and in a very good way – I was very fortunate to attract the greatest gift, my now wife, into my life after this transformation.

The point is that adhering exactly to the recommended guidelines is probably the only way you are going to get real and lasting health and happiness benefits. Small reductions in exposure to toxic foods is only likely to be helpful if it is a stepping stone to complete adherence to the recommended guidelines. This is one reason why so few people reap the benefits of a really healthy diet; many people are still messing around making minor modifications to a toxic diet. And while you are still indulging in fizzy drinks and other unhealthy foods the chances are high that you will eventually return to them in full force.

I make no apologies for the fact that you might need to completely overhaul your lifestyle. The reality is that the biggest changes to unhealthy lifestyles generate the greatest benefits, physically and mentally, as well as financially. Remember this: all of the lifestyle recommendations I have made in this book are not just protective against pain, injuries, vascular disease, dementia and cognitive decline – they will move you towards your ultimate health and happiness, with an asset of unstoppable energy to share your gifts with the world.

The good news is that our brain and bodies are learning machines and they will react to how they are treated.

If we optimise our thoughts, daily activities and behaviours – we will live a kickass life! But if we leave our bodies sitting on a chair or couch, and live a sedentary lifestyle – our brain and bodies will severely lack energy and our muscle performance will swiftly decrease. Combine this with our food and fluid intake: we are either poisoning our brain and bodies with toxins from processed and artificial foods – it's like eating cancer, dementia or disease – or we are enriching our brain and bodies with essential nutrients.

Lets pause for a moment – what will you decide – to make this principle work for you or against you? I know you have many meaningful reasons to make it work for you!

After working with thousands of people from all different backgrounds over the past decade – there is generally a destructive assumption made, typically from those who are over 50 years of age. From my experience people usually do get less active as they age – because they have a strong belief and outmoded concept of retirement. Other factors may include injuries, motivation, careers, and attitudes. But perhaps the decline after we reach retirement age is testimony to the ill-effects of retirement versus the inevitability of cognitive decline with age? With a lack of use our brain, body, and organs decline at any age. There are many compelling examples of people of advanced years, who continue with active lifestyles, and continue to do amazing things, like run marathons and contribute significantly to public life. But you don't have to be that fit – just staying functional, and testing your body regularly in a safe manner – will enable you to enjoy more years of quality life.

However, we expect that the above elements of our health are going to deteriorate and that we have little control over the process. That is simply incorrect! We have a lot of influence about how we age, even if we have no power to stop the fact that we age.

How to Make Behaviour Changes

Behaviour change is not about knowing what to do. Most people know they need to exercise regularly, eat a natural plant-based diet with minimal or no processed or fried food, but they don't adhere to these guidelines. The fact is that behaviour change is much less about knowing, or thinking, than it is doing. You literally have to reprogram and rewire your brain and body, and that involves work. However, as I have mentioned all along, small continuous changes are the key to maintained behaviour change. The emphasis being on *maintained* behaviour change. There is no point on going on an unsustainable program to lose weight. You might lose weight (i.e. reach your outcome) – in the short term – but you're not learning, or retraining your brain and body.

The key is to make change efforts that can be sustained and build on them. For example, I have had clients who started an exercise program by walking a couple of hundred metres to the end of their street and back. Gradually, they extended the distance as their confidence and fitness increased and now several of them are running a few kilometres, four days a week. However, if they started out with the idea of running a few kilometres, they might have never got off the couch.

It is important to think about developing new habits rather than trying to get rid of old ones. I want you to focus on developing health rather than trying to change bad habits. The emphasis needs to be on the new, healthy activities you are doing and choices that you are making. What this means is that you need to select manageable goals that you can achieve in the present and see them as stepping-stones to greater health and control. In fact, a ladder metaphor is useful. Each step you take on the ladder takes you closer to the one above it and nearer to your overall goal. Ensure you celebrate each step you take with a victory dance – it will train your brain to seek more of it!

So, the first principle is to start with small manageable behaviours that can be maintained constantly. In order to achieve these, you need to be able to identify and state exactly what those goals are. For example, walk fifteen minutes a day, don't sit for longer than twenty minutes at a time, eat no fried food today, and so on.

There are five other crucial factors, which will determine your success at changing behaviour and ultimately transforming your life forever.

1. **Support.** It is much easier to adopt new behaviours if the people around you, especially those you live with, are not only supportive of your efforts, but are actually engaging in the positive behaviours you aspire to. We are heavily influenced by the behaviours of others, especially those in our immediate environment and we can observe what they are doing. So it is important you enlist support from others to help you. That support could be informal or more formal, like a support group, or a bike-riding group. In addition, support offers you accountability. It's easy to blow off an important activity like a workout session, if you are the only one who knows you have postponed it. If you are serious about making real changes, hire a quality health and fitness professional, potentially the greatest support you will ever receive and the best investment you will ever make. The best changes in my life would not have occurred with out my coaches, mentors, trainers and teachers – I will be forever grateful for each one of them for their time, energy, knowledge and care.

2. **Mindfulness.** It is very easy to go along on auto-pilot, not realising what you are doing at the time, or at the very least paying it proper attention. So it is critical that you have ways of monitoring your behaviour be that an app, or a journal or some other device. Obviously, monitoring a behaviour makes you focus on it, and often that itself can be enough to create change.

3. **Time.** One of the biggest excuses for not making important behavioural changes is time. Sure, many of us live busy lives, but it is up to each of us to determine our priorities. In fact, many of the changes don't take up much time at all, or any more time than unhealthier alternatives. The exception might be exercise, but given that exercise often energises us, one could argue that you are going to get some of that time back in the form of extra energy to do other activities.

4. **Stress.** The toxic element in stress is being out of control and when you feel that way, the chances are that even your best-laid plans are going to be derailed. Ironically, it is exactly when we are stressed that we need to adopt healthy behaviours. We need to exercise, eat healthily, get good sleep and relax, all of which we are least likely to do when stressed. It is why stress obliteration and relaxation are such important skills – they can prevent bad situations from getting worse.

5. **Preparation**. You need to ensure you have the materials and things you need to be able to make the changes you have planned. For example, do you have the right workout clothing? Do you have a journal and/or an app or computer program in which to record your progress?

Planning on these variables is important. In summary, you need to:

- Know exactly what small new behaviour you are trying to implement

- Know how and when you are going to do it
- Gather support to make it more likely
- Monitor your behaviour
- Not allow stress to derail you
- Ensure you have the resources that you need
- Repeat the behaviour on a regular, ideally daily, basis.

The four key lifestyle areas that are critical to your health and happiness are:

- Nutrition
- Exercise
- Mindfulness/Stress obliteration
- Sleep

The next step is to download your free Wescombe Method 42-Day Kick Starters Guide (valued at $150) via www.BestBody.com.au/bookbonus – it has been designed to create a strong foundation to launch behavioural changes in a sustainable way that will move you towards your ultimate health and happiness.

Now, the one thing I would love to hear about is your success story – hearing personal success stories will never get old for me. You can connect with me on Instagram @scottwescombe or on Facebook. Also follow along on the Best Body blog. You can also reach me at scott@bestbody.com.au

I genuinely look forward to meeting you face to face someday, but until then focus on the actions that will take you down the rich pathway towards a meaningful, healthy and happy life. Now is the time for you to step up and unleash the deepest driving force of life within you!

About the Author

Scott Wescombe

Author, Entrepreneur, Physiotherapist, Trainer, and Public Speaker

Scott is an author, coach, entrepreneur, physiotherapist, certified body trainer and public speaker.

Having grown up in the family health business, Scott has worked for more than a decade in the health and fitness industry, owning and operating several health-related businesses over the years. Eager to make a mark in his field, he opened his first physiotherapy practice immediately after earning his Bachelor of Science in Exercise and Sports Science and his Bachelor of Science in Physiotherapy with first class honours.

In addition to his university degrees, Scott is a certified Strategic Life Coach, certified Les Mills Body Trainer and holds a Diploma of Exercise Science and Fitness Management as well as a Certificate 3 and Certificate 4 in Fitness. He has used his formal training and industry experience to coach other health business owners and as a guest lecturer for Sports Medicine Australia.

Currently the owner of Best Body, Scott runs on sheer drive and relentless vision. His love for fitness and his competitive nature goes back to his childhood where he spent countless hours watching his father coach runners and sprinters. An athletic superstar in his own right, Scott broke multiple state junior records. In addition to playing basketball, he played football in the AFL National U/18 Championships. He also played for the Subiaco Football Club in the WAFL.

Scott's professional associations include the Australian Physiotherapy Association and Sports Medicine Australia.

He has traveled and worked throughout New Zealand, Chile, Argentina, Brazil, Paraguay, Indonesia, Thailand, Singapore, UAE, France, Italy, Croatia, Montenegro, the United Kingdom, Spain, Portugal, Norway, Sweden, Denmark, Netherlands, Canada, the United States, Mexico, Germany, Greece and Turkey.

Scott Wescombe is the author of *From Pain & Injury to Healthy & Happy* and lives in Western Australia.

Resources

Resources

Best Body

Best Body is a private organisation created to empower individuals to live a better quality of life for longer through superior health and happiness. The Best Body family, which consists of super passionate health professionals and incredible support stars, has a vision of instigating people to be happy daily. The Wescombe Method provides a proven pathway for people to live an extraordinary life – to move from pain & injury to healthy & happy – where the individual is healthier and happier in all aspects of life, close relationships are revived and thriving, and success becomes a habit. It is a method with a results guarantee, and many individuals receive rapid and transformational results.

What began as one man's individual effort to deliver a better health service and transform people's lives has now grown into a movement. The establishment was built on the belief that every person deserves the same high level of care and honesty that would be provided to a family member or loved one. Through providing genuine education, leadership, support, accountability, connection, and inspiration Best Body is looking to have a global impact with your help.

All of the author's profits from this book '*From Pain & Injury To Healthy & Happy*' will be donated to Manna, a volunteer driven charity in Western Australia focused on feeding and serving the homeless. Find out more about Manna or make a donation via www.manna.org.au

www.BestBody.com.au